WORK PREPARATION FOR THE HANDICAPPED

CROOM HELM SPECIAL EDUCATION SERIES
Edited by Bill Gillham, Child Development Research Unit,
University of Nottingham

Already Available:

ENCOURAGING LANGUAGE DEVELOPMENT
Phyllis Hastings and Bessie Hayes

INDEPENDENCE TRAINING FOR VISUALLY HANDICAPPED
CHILDREN
Doris W. Tooze

WORK PREPARATION FOR THE HANDICAPPED
David Hutchinson

Scheduled for Publication in Early 1982:

TOYS AND PLAY FOR THE HANDICAPPED CHILD
Barbara Riddick

DAILY LIVING WITH THE HANDICAPPED CHILD
Diana Millard

TEACHING POOR READERS IN THE SECONDARY SCHOOL
Christine Cassell

Work Preparation for the Handicapped

David Hutchinson

CROOM HELM LONDON

© 1982 David Hutchinson
Croom Helm Ltd, 2-10 St John's Road, London SW11

British Library Cataloguing in Publication Data

Hutchinson, David
    Work preparation for the handicapped – (Croom
    Helm special education series)
    1. Handicapped – Employment – Great Britain
    2. Vocational guidance – Great Britain
    I. Title
    371.9   LC4036.G7

    ISBN 0–7099–0283–2

Filmset by Leaper and Gard Ltd, Bristol
Printed and bound in Great Britain
 by Billing and Sons Limited
Guildford, London, Oxford, Worcester

Contents

Tables and Figures

Series Foreword

The Croom Helm Special Education Series is explicitly intended to give experienced practitioners in the helping services the opportunity to present a wide range of remedial programmes and techniques which they have developed in practice. The basis of the editorial policy is the belief that there exists much 'good practice' which warrants wider dissemination in book form so that its influence can extend beyond the local area where it is established. The present project is, therefore, concerned with the communication of ideas and methods developed by those who use them in their working lives.

Work Preparation for the Handicapped deals with the practical problems of helping young handicapped people towards a fuller life by preparing them for a role in the working community.

B.G.

Preface

Work preparation for the handicapped is not a new area of provision and has been with us for a period of time stretching back to the Great War. In recent years, however, it has developed a new facet in the form of work preparation courses for handicapped young people as a part of further education, a development given impetus by the publication of the Warnock Report, *Special Educational Needs*, in 1978. Warnock suggested a national co-ordinated programme to extend the present advisory, training and placement services in order that the reserves of skill and talent existing amongst handicapped people might be developed to the extent that they could play a positive and independent role in society to the benefit of that society in both human and material terms.

Encouraging statements have to be backed up by the detailed planning of training programmes in the context of existing provision. This book, therefore, has two objectives:

(1) To describe what work preparation facilities are available to handicapped young people for the increasing number of those interested in this field (including the young people concerned and their parents).
(2) To provide information for those involved in planning work preparation courses for the handicapped in Colleges of Further Education or elsewhere and, where these are established, to suggest how they might be improved.

The book is not intended to be prescriptive, but to sketch in the background to current developments and to offer guidelines for future expansion.

Acknowledgements

Thanks are due to the following for their encouragement and support in the preparation of this book: Norman C. Clegg, Principal, North Nottinghamshire College of Further Education; Terence Taylor, Deputy Head of the Work Orientation Unit, and the Unit Staff, past and present; George Cooke, Dennis Coe and other colleagues on the Warnock Post–16s Sub–committee; and my wife Janet and my family.

Sam Grainger took all the photographs 'on site' in the Unit; Dennis Vardy produced the diagrams; and the final draft was materially improved with the help of the Series Editor, Bill Gillham.

I would like to acknowledge the following for permission to derive from copyright figures: R.J. Andrews and the Education Research Centre, University of Queensland (Figure 1.1); S. Mattingley and Update Publications Ltd. (Figure 1.2); Manpower Services Commission (Figure 1.3).

D.H.

CHAPTER 1

Basic Considerations

'Work is an essential part of a man's life, since it is that aspect of his life which gives him status and binds him to society.'[1]

'Our readiness to accept any disabled person's right to work on whatever terms he can offer must be seen as the touch-stone of our acceptance of him as a full member of the human race.'[2]

The notions of 'the work ethic' and 'positive discrimination' reflected in these statements can still be considered as basic tenets of our society. To be able to work is a symbol of full social status, but many handicapped people are faced with the *probability* of not being able to obtain permanent work and so being reduced to a lifelong dependency on others. Despite the realistic pessimism about open market employment prospects in a time of economic recession, it remains valid to say that the idea of positive discrimination in favour of the handicapped in employment has still to be explored fully. This implies an allocation of resources, specifically ear-marked for the purpose, if every handicapped person is to have an opportunity to make his best contribution in so far as his abilities will allow, and for him to have maximum possible job satisfaction with a commensurate degree of independence. What, then, is the current situation as far as the handicapped school-leaver is concerned, and how could it be improved?

Numbers

Of the total number of handicapped people seeking employment, the smallest group is that made up of young people whose handicap is congenital or acquired early in life. In many ways it is the very size of this group that has caused their problems to be ignored by the responsible authorities who have developed services with other groups of handicapped people in mind. The numbers of young people leaving special schools and units in England and Wales are fewer than 8,000 per year and these present a range of physical, sensory, intellectual and emotional difficulties at various levels. The handicaps can be multiple, more or less complex, and progressive or variable in nature. The total number can also be added to at any time by those who experience some form of traumatic injury, for example as a result of road traffic accidents, thus increasing the range and difficulty of problems.

If the Warnock Report's[3] assumptions of 'about one in six children at any time, and up to one in five children at some time' requiring some form of special education provision are valid, then there are probably many more 'handi-capped' young people leaving ordinary schools each year than leave special schools. The implications of this are significant, for unless the level of services provided by local authorities to the handicapped in ordinary schools is just as high as that provided to those in special schools, then such children will be absorbed into the local number of school-leavers (as, indeed, they are at the moment), which makes their numbers difficult to estimate and their needs difficult to meet. Nevertheless, not all such school-leavers become 'lost' to the system; some, not identified at 16 years of age, do appear at a later date after a period of unemployment, perhaps when applying to be registered as a disabled person.

The Need for Further Education and Training

In 1964 a working party under the chairmanship of Dr Elfed Thomas, at that time Director of Education for Leicester, reported that 'many handicapped young people are engaged in unrewarding, routine employment solely because it was work they were able to do without further training and that, given a better education to fit them for a course of training, they might well have derived all the added satisfaction that goes with skilled employment'.[4] The need for further education and training provision for handicapped young people was examined by Tuckey *et al.* in 1973[5] in a study of 788 school-leavers. Their findings may be summarised as shown in Table 1.1.

Table 1.1 indicates one aspect of the dual problem facing the handicapped in seeking employment, namely lack of training and/or further education, which leads to under-employment in work often well below the individual's potential. The same report further identified the problem of unemployment, currently at a high level amongst the normal school-leaving population but traditionally high amongst handicapped school-leavers (see Table 1.2).

However, these figures do not reveal the complexity of the problem which is shown by examining in more detail the experience of those who *are* employed (see Table 1.3).

One of the problems of the handicapped school-leaving population is that the percentage of that group categorised as ESN(S) or ESN(M)[a] (two out of every

Note: a. In the US, trainable or educable mental retardates.

Table 1.1: Suitability for Further Education, Higher Education and Training

Category disability	% suitable for FE/HE	% suitable for FE/HE and training who actually received it	% suitable for training only who actually received it
Blind	93	50	74
Partially-sighted	89	47	44
Physically-handicapped	95	40	33
Maladjusted	76	29	27
Deaf	86	23	24
Epileptic	70	20	20
ESN	86	9	16
All n = 788	83	34	27

Source: After Tuckey *et al.*, 1973.

Table 1.2: Percentage in Each Handicapped Group who had ever Worked

Category of disability	% who had ever worked
Blind	37
Partially-sighted	72
Physically-handicapped	65
Maladjusted	97
Deaf	92
Epileptic	82
ESN	86
All n = 788	76

Source: After Tuckey *et al.*, 1973.

Table 1.3: Employment Experiences of Five Groups of Handicapped School-leavers

Group	% who had ever worked	Open employment	Sheltered employment	First job 1+ yrs (%)	Average no. of jobs per person	Un-employed for 6+ months (%)
Partially-sighted	72 (n = 39)	38	1	31	2.4	23
Deaf	92 (n = 83)	82	1	51	1.9	17
ESN	86 (n = 249)	204	43	35	2.4	11
Physically-handicapped	65 (n = 161)	120	37	30	1.9	30
Maladjusted	97 (n = 34)	34	—	30	4.2	15

Source: After Tuckey *et al.*, 1973.

three). The research project on the employment of handicapped school-leavers commissioned by the Warnock Committee,[6] which began its work in 1975 and finished in 1977, did in fact have relatively high numbers of young people in these categories as part of its sample and is, therefore, relevant to the discussion at this point. The project had two main aims:

'to explore the reasons for the success or failure of handicapped young people to get or keep a job'; and

'to obtain some indication of the extent of unused capacity for employment up to the age of about 18 years, together with a consideration of further education, training and of family and other support'.

The sample of young people was obtained from the National Child Development Study,[7] which has followed the progress of all children in Britain born in one week in March 1958. Four groups of young people were identified from the sample:

(1) *The handicapped group* – those formally ascertained as needing special education, the majority of whom had been in special schools or units at 16.
(2) *The 'special help' group* – those receiving help for educational backwardness but who were not formally ascertained.
(3) *The 'would benefit' group* – those not formally ascertained nor receiving special help at the age of 16, but who in the opinion of their teachers would have benefited from this.
(4) *The non-handicapped group* – a control group with no apparent handicap nor need for special help at 16.

The survey was based upon structured interviews and the results presented as follows (Table 1.4):

Table 1.4: Percentage of Handicapped and Non-handicapped Young People Working or not Working at the Time of the Interview

| | Sample group | |
Current employment status	Ascertained as handicapped	Non-handicapped (control group)
Employed	47.8	66.4
Unemployed – seeking work	19.1	4.4
– not seeking work	8.0	—
Still at school or in further education	5.6	29.2
Adult training centre or sheltered workshop	14.7	—
Other (in hospital/borstal)	4.8	—
Total	100	100
(Number)	(251)	(113)

Source: from Warnock Research Project, 1977.

The findings of the research project confirmed that a higher percentage of the non-handicapped was in employment and that greater numbers of the non-handicapped were in more skilled occupations; in the industrial sector, at least, handicapped young people were more likely to be engaged in lower level work. In terms of unemployment, rather more than twice as many of them faced some unemployment and, over a period of two years, ten times as many handicapped young people had been out of work for six months or more than the non-handicapped who had left full-time education. Any improvements, therefore, in the situation facing handicapped school-leavers will depend to a great extent on further education and vocational training opportunities to improve skills and relevant qualifications.

The Type of Provision Available

Assessment

A realistic assessment of the handicapped young person at a time well before the school-leaving date is required if hasty preparation and mis-match work placements are to be avoided. The need for assessment is met in a number of interesting ways by local authorities and voluntary organisations. A number of schools have developed their own programmes designed to meet their own needs. A good illustration of this is provided by an ESN(M) school in Gravesend where, through a variety of structured activities and experiences carefully monitored by staff, young people are encouraged to become aware of their strengths and weaknesses. Other establishments use a multi-professional approach; for example, the Young Persons' Work Preparation Course conducted at the *Employment Rehabilitation Centre* in Sheffield. This type of approach is made possible because instructors, a teacher, a social worker, an occupational psychologist and medical staff are part of the professional team at the centre. Additionally, the specialist careers officer for the local authority is closely involved in the initial selection and continuing assessment of the young people and their placement at the end of the course. Approximately 80 per cent of all Employment Rehabilitation Centres have such courses, but the Employment Service Agency has the objective of raising the number of places available from the 1976 level of 550 to 1,000 places in 1980–81, and to cover all ERCs.

There is no doubt as to the value of these courses in terms of providing vocational assessment and initial training over a limited period of time (normally twelve weeks) and this is measured by the success of the trainees in obtaining employment. However, some handicapped school-leavers will require a much more detailed kind of assessment covering more than vocational elements and, perhaps, extending over a longer period. Such provision has been made available fairly recently by the Queen Elizabeth's Foundation for the Disabled at Banstead Place. Here, residential assessment and training facilities are available for those with severe physical handicaps, often compounded by immaturity. Previously, the needs of this group have not been met and in many cases the young people were regarded as untrainable and unemployable.

Provision for the assessment of handicapped school-leavers is very uneven and not available in many parts of the country. Warnock[8] stresses the need for a continuous dialogue between a comprehensive team of specialists, including the school and the careers service, together with the young person and his parents. This is a reasonable objective and may require no more than the better organisation of existing services rather than the development of new ones.

Before leaving the question of assessment at this introductory level it is necessary to sound a cautionary note. Assessment is a term currently in vogue in the everyday vocabulary of education and training services, but subject to a good deal of misinterpretation, even misuse. The concept of assessment often appears to be narrowly defined in terms of a set process taking place over a given time after which a set of valid results and predictions can be made. Rather, it should be seen as a flexible, on-going process, based ideally upon the evaluation of clearly established aims and objectives from which gradually emerges a picture where further possible activities are revealed. Too often, the nature of assessment processes is limited to the formal aspects and insufficient attention paid to the *functional* role of assessment. We return to this theme in Chapter 3.

Education and Training   .

The basis for the development of employment potential in the handicapped lies mainly in the educational programmes open to them. Education, in the broadest sense, would include the full development of cognitive, motor and emotional potential as the basis upon which the handicapped young person could proceed to work adjustment and adult life in general. The minimum programme to ensure optimum employment opportunities for the handicapped also requires work training and placement, and follow-up services that preferably are not appendages to educational programmes but separate programmes available to those who need them: essentially a flexible pattern of progression from education to employment, as outlined in Figure 1.1. This is derived from the model suggested by Andrews (1976),[9] based upon research carried out in Australia. Essentially six areas of activity are suggested providing a variety of educational and vocational experience with linking pathways which are an indispensable element in the model. The subsequent discussion on the areas of activity will be confined to broad principles and areas of concern only. One area, that of *further education*, will not feature at this stage, but will form the substance of Chapter 2.

Figure 1.1: A Model of Flexible Progression from Education to Employment

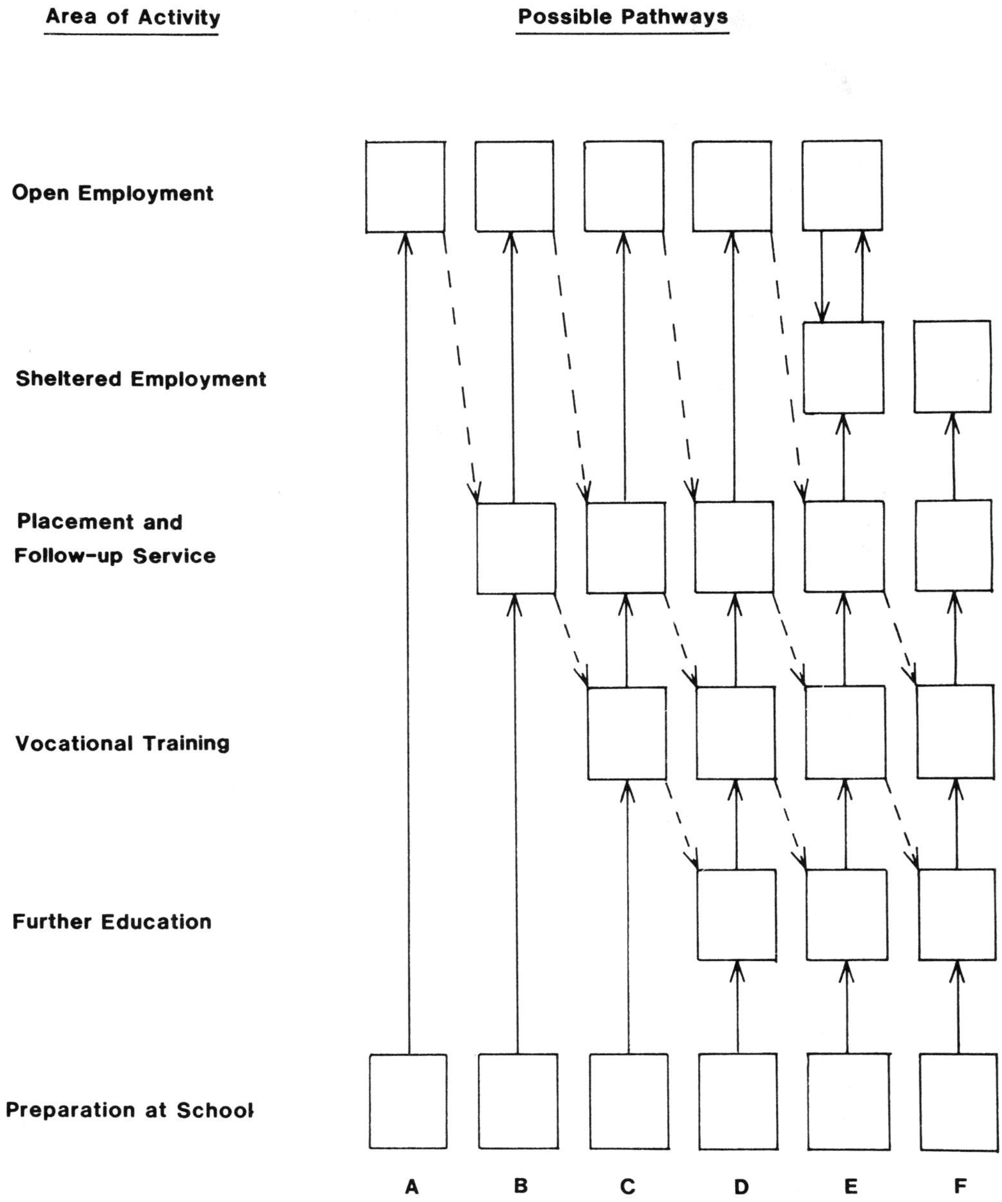

Area of Activity   **Possible Pathways**

Open Employment

Sheltered Employment

**Placement and
Follow-up Service**

Vocational Training

Further Education

Preparation at School

A   B   C   D   E   F

Source: After Andrews, 1976.

From Education to Employment

Preparation at School

Special schools have an important role to play in providing handicapped pupils with the appropriate degree of independence required to cope with open employment. However, the evidence available from further education and vocational training establishments leads to the conclusion that many handicapped school-leavers have inadequate attainment in basic subjects, and only minimal levels of social competence, ill-equipping them to meet the demands of adult and working life. Certainly, the protective environment of a special school can make it difficult to prepare young people for employment; such factors as the length of the school day, the restricted curriculum and all-age schools do not assist the school-leaver in preparing for adult life. Also, some will require more education than that generally allowed for by present school-leaving practices in order to reach their best level of work adjustment.

The school is still, of course, a powerful agent in the shaping of attitudes and expectations amongst school-leavers, and in the later years at school the curriculum must focus on the needs of children in the adult world in terms of life and social skills. Of significance, therefore, is the development of link courses between schools and colleges and, also, the extension of experience via the Education Work Experience Act 1973. Both of these facilities now mean that many young handicapped people regularly spend periods of time in further education colleges or on industrial premises. These links can enable the young people concerned to widen their personal, educational and vocational horizons – but not if the placements are too narrowly focused on vocational skills and are not closely integrated with work undertaken at school.

Some handicapped sixteen-year-olds may benefit from remaining longer at school. Legislative authority is given for this by the various Education Acts and may well be facilitated by the current experience of many schools with falling rolls. However, in the development of these 'sixth forms', special schools have to exercise care in planning courses to ensure that the curriculum really extends and develops pupils and that it does not become a mere 'holding operation' or an exercise in maintaining school numbers. In placing handicapped young people on continuation courses at school, bearing in mind the possible limitations of special schools referred to above, it is important to consider what opportunities already exist in alternative post-16 educational establishments. In times of scarce resources, duplication of provision can be avoided by comprehensive structured planning at the local level.

Vocational Training

For many handicapped young people, the traditional route into employment has been via vocational training and this remains true today. Many of those who have trained in this way have acquired their skills at one of the four *Residential Training Colleges:* Portland Training College, Mansfield, Nottinghamshire; Finchale Training College, Durham; Queen Elizabeth's Training College, Leatherhead, Surrey; St Loye's Training College, Exeter, Devon. The range of training courses available is extensive and continues to develop. In total, there are approximately 800 places and many trainees are funded by the Training Services Division of the Manpower Services Commission or by Local Education Authorities. (Some idea of the range of courses available at these colleges can be found in Appendix 1.)

Additionally, further training facilities have been developed by *voluntary bodies* in response to the particular needs of a specific handicapped group, for example:

(1)	For the blind—	The Royal College for the Blind, Hereford
		Heathersett Centre for the Blind, Reigate, Surrey
		Queen Alexandra College, Birmingham
(2)	For the deaf—	The Sir James E. Jones School of Vocational Training, Manchester
(3)	For the ESN(S)—	Lufton Manor, Somerset
		Coleg Elidyr, Mid Wales
		Pengwern Hall, North Wales
(4)	For the ESN(M) —	Derwen College for the Disabled, Oswestry, Shropshire (as part of its normal work)
(5)	For the physically-handicapped —	Beaumont College, Lancaster
		National Star Centre, Cheltenham

This form of training has pioneered the way for many handicapped young people to obtain necessary qualifications and skills for employment, and the results achieved over the years have been very impressive. Whilst many centres were established initially to provide vocational training only, latterly they have become involved in more comprehensive education because of the demand. This illustrates the way in which voluntary bodies can reveal the inadequacies of the state system. Nevertheless, this type of provision is not without its inherent problems, for example:

the high cost of providing and maintaining residential placement;
the high cost of selection criteria for admission to some course places which excludes many handicapped school-leavers;
the long distance and remoteness, in terms of easy communication, from the

trainees' home areas (often a problem with residential schools), which creates difficulties in the maintenance of support;
limitations placed on the range of training which does not always reflect the employment possibilities available in the trainees' home areas.

The second main provision of training for the handicapped has come from the *Manpower Services Commission* through its two executive branches, the *Employment Services Division* and the *Training Services Division*. Part of the work of the Employment Services Division (ESD) has already been referred to (see p. 5), where the twelve-week courses at Employment Rehabilitation Centres (ERCs) were described. The ERC with its national network of 26 centres provides a facility which many young handicapped people make use of, though the primary intention is to provide vocational guidance and industrial rehabilitation for those who have become disabled because of sickness or injury. Figure 1.2 (from Mattingley)[10] illustrates the type of experience provided by an ERC and indicates the multi-disciplinary approach.

It is not the intention of an ERC to train handicapped people for skilled work, but approximately 25 per cent do go on to vocational training elsewhere. More than 14,000 people per year pass through the ERC courses, 65 per cent are in work or training, and 5 to 10 per cent more have done some work; obviously the general employment outlook in an area will affect placements in work. Whilst most ERCs attempt to simulate an industrial environment and are non-resident, some do have residential facilities and others are associated with hospitals to encourage links between the health and employment services. An example of this is provided by the ERC opened in 1974 at the Queen Elizabeth Medical Centre in Birmingham.

The Training Services Division (TSD) is prepared to fund handicapped people in courses at Residential Training Colleges, but it also operates its own vocational training centres in the shape of 60 *Skills Centres*. Courses generally last for six months and help is given to obtain work. Although many of the 50 or so trades offered are not suitable for the handicapped, some are, for example:

carpentry	capstan setting
watch/clock repairing	milling
typewriter repairing	centre-lathe turning
instrument fitting/machining	welding
motor vehicle repair	radio/television repair
spray painting	electronic wiring
circuit testing	

One of the major TSD contributions towards training, particularly for those who have been unable to obtain it earlier in life, has been the *Training Opportunities Scheme* (TOPS). There are over 800 different kinds of TOPS Courses and whilst they are intended to provide workers with new vocational skills,

Figure 1.2: The Organisation of Employment Rehabilitation Centres

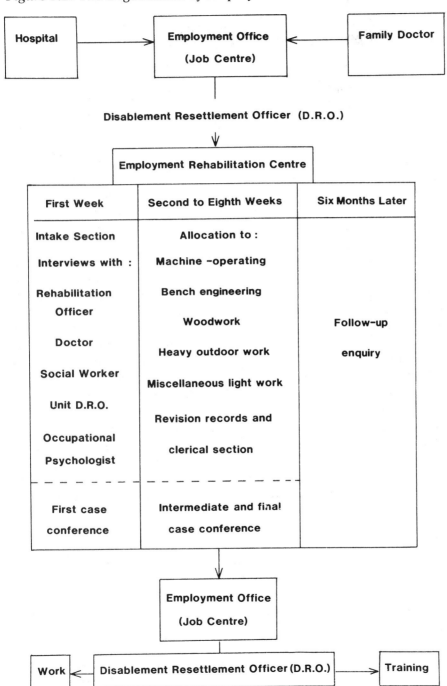

Source: From Mattingley, 1977.

many are also suitable for the handicapped; examples of these are provided by both craft training and limited-skills training in engineering, electronics, clerical and commercial work. TOPS training can be undertaken on either an exclusive or an in-fill basis at Skills Centres, Colleges of Further Education and Residential Training Colleges. In general, the courses last from three to twelve months and the minimum age is 19 years, though discretion may be exercisd in favour of a lower age of entry. In discussions on TOPS training which took place as part of the Warnock Committee's work,[11] it was found that the numbers of handicapped people on TSD courses was low, though the evidence to support this view was difficult to obtain and the suggested reasons complex. Nevertheless, it does remain a cause for concern bearing in mind the extent of TSD training, especially TOPS.

The 1974 report *Unqualified, Untrained and Unemployed*[12] indicated that a high proportion of young handicapped people lacked educational qualifications and were recommended for jobs offering little or no training. This creates a double disadvantage for, in addition to a handicap, they fare badly in competition with other young people at a level where the job market is very competitive anyway. As a result, the Report found that they remained unemployed, on average, for twice as long as other young people and that when they did manage to obtain work, about 82 per cent were given jobs offering no prospects or training. In the light of the evidence presented, it would be quite wrong to assume that the handicapped will benefit to any great extent from so-called 'normal' schemes designed to relieve youth unemployment in general; a measure of positive discrimination would seem to be called for.

With this in mind we must consider the effect of the 1977 report *Young People at Work* (The Holland Report),[13] which led to the launching of one of the Manpower Services Commission's special programmes – the *Youth Opportunities Programme* – on 1 April 1978. The aim of this programme is to offer the young unemployed opportunities for training and work experience that will improve their prospects of obtaining a satisfactory permanent job at the earliest possible moment, and provide a constructive alternative to unemployment. Although reference was made in early documentation to the needs of those with lower ability, the Youth Opportunities Programme did not at the outset cater specifically for handicapped young people. Indeed, it was suggested by the Manpower Services Commission, in offering guidance in courses for the less able, that the lowest level of ability for which preparation could be made for ordinary unsheltered employment was ESN(M), and that those who had more severe problems should be directed to education courses run by Local Education Authorities. Following pressure from many sources the scope of the provision was widened to include, amongst others, those with physical handicaps, the ESN(S), the maladjusted and those with sensory handicaps. In addition, an individual young person might be allowed to remain on a course for 26 weeks, though introductory courses are normally of 13 weeks duration and, if a course is so designed to meet the needs of a particular disadvantaged group, consideration can be given to allowing the course to run for 26 weeks.

Inevitably, as the number of available jobs has fallen and the Youth Opportunities Programme has grown, more and more handicapped school-leavers have been taken on. This prompted the Manpower Services Commission to publish a leaflet *Special Programmes, Special Needs* in February 1980, looking at the facts and implications of unemployment amongst the handicapped and offering examples of how the Youth Opportunities Programme has helped. However, the Programme should, of course, be seen as a general measure to deal with youth unemployment and it would be inappropriate to see it as a long-term solution to the problems of unemployment and under-employment amongst the handicapped. The Youth Opportunities Programme is, therefore, complementary to the proposals of the Warnock Report, not an alternative. There is a danger that financial incentives for both students and colleges could lead to inappropriate provision on the one hand and no provision at all for those who really need it on the other.

Placement and Follow-up Service

Warnock[14] reinforces the vital need at the education-employment interface for a specialist, a 'named person', to act as co-ordinator and counsellor to help the young handicapped person negotiate the difficult, often unmarked, pathways that lie ahead. In suggesting that the *specialist careers officer* should fulfil this 'named person' role, the Report raises implications for the careers service, not least the case-load carried by these officers and, indeed, the very number of them. Recommendation 12:2 of the Warnock Report gives a general guideline that at least one full-time specialist careers officer should be appointed for every 50,000 of the school population. Although most Local Education Authorities would claim to have specialist careers officers, in many cases this can be on a part-time basis with one officer covering a large geographical or population area: clearly an unsatisfactory state of affairs bearing in mind the need for regular contact, especially where the child is attending a residential school away from home. The careers officer needs to be closely involved with the school and requires help and support from careers teachers in the school.

The needs of the handicapped feature as part of the basic training of careers officers. With the increasing number of handicapped children in ordinary schools, this is clearly important; but there is also a need for some form of specialist post-experience training, perhaps along the lines of that currently available to *disablement resettlement officers*. This latter service is part of the Employment Services Division's function and a disablement resettlement officer can be found at most job centres and employment offices. In each area there is a number of senior officers and resettlement advisers, which gives some career prospects to those seeking promotion but who do not wish to leave the area of work. None the less, lack of opportunities for promotion are a problem, as with the careers service, and the need for career enhancement may cause both specialists to go off in other directions within the service. A national disablement resettlement officer training centre has now been established and, following routine employment adviser training, a minimum of ten weeks special training in the needs of the handicapped is given to all disablement resettlement officers.

The role of the placement and follow-up services in the preparation of the handicapped for employment is complex. At the heart of the matter is good communications between all the agencies involved. Figure 1.3 summarises the interdependence of these different services.

Sheltered Employment

Whilst the objective for most young handicapped people would be to get a job in open employment, it has to be recognised that for many severely handicapped people this is not feasible. Thus sheltered workshops provide an answer for the employment needs of some of these young people, though such workshops are few and are subject to the vagaries of market conditions.

Sheltered employment is provided traditionally in three ways: by *Remploy*, by *local authorities* and by *voluntary organisations*. Remploy was set up in 1946 by the government as a non-profit making body. Today it has 89 factories in a national network and over 8,000 disabled employees, making it the largest employer of the disabled. Many of those working with young congenitally handicapped people feel that it is more difficult to place this group in Remploy than it is to place normal workers who become disabled through accident or injury – reflecting the original purpose of Remploy to provide work for the war disabled.

Rather fewer handicapped people are employed in sheltered workshops run by local authorities and provision of this type tends to vary both in quality and quantity from region to region. Much of the work undertaken tends to be of the unskilled routine type that is becoming difficult to obtain with increasing mechanisation. Some of the more imaginative sheltered workshops are run by voluntary bodies and include some with residential facilities for married couples. For example, three of the bodies responsible for Residential Training Colleges, Queen Elizabeth's, Portland and St Loye's, also run sheltered workshops.

Most sheltered workshops appear to have financial problems and experience difficulty in obtaining work, though some have developed their own product lines quite successfully as an alternative to sub-contract work from industry. It is clear that these workshops are necessary as part of the employment provision for handicapped people, but greater flexibility is needed to make possible a transfer to open employment for those who are capable, and to enhance job satisfaction for those who are not. If this sort of provision is to develop, more financial backing is required from government, perhaps in co-operation with industry, local authorities and the voluntary bodies.

Figure 1.3: The Role of the Placement and Follow-up Services

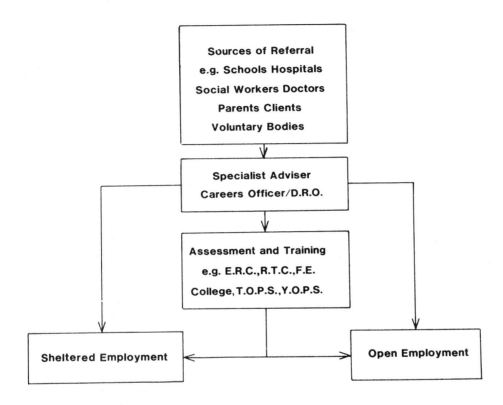

Open Employment

In seeking open employment the handicapped do not differ from the normal population, neither do they seek different forms of work satisfaction. Occupational satisfaction is difficult to define and is a theme to which we shall return in Chapter 3. It can be thought of as comprising a number of elements, which include:

significance   continuity
financial rewards   intrinsic interest

achievement	advancement
social status	self-improvement
security	social interaction

The twin problems of under-employment and unemployment often frustrate the handicapped in seeking occupational goals and can be added to by low expectations on the part of parents and professionals and, to some extent, handicapped people themselves. The present economic situation might lead us to think that employment is the particular reserve of the able-bodied and that for many people with handicaps work is an unattainable objective. Indeed, there are those who believe that the handicapped are incapable of surviving in the world of work and are unsuited to the maintenance of a life of positive economic performance. Lowman (1977)[15] states:

> there can be little place for concepts like protected work or sympathetic employers since at this difficult interface between human and material resources, economic reality always wins in the end. What is the key to much more success for the handicapped in employment lies in the realisation for all concerned that they are individuals with ambitions and possibilities just like anyone else and that they can, and do, contribute positively to the economic criteria of the organisation for whom they work.

An industrialist with a special interest in the employment of the handicapped, Lowman has taken the consideration of open employment out of the realms of sympathy or apprehension, to one of using and developing individual abilities.

Over the years, successive governments have attempted to alter the environment in favour of the handicapped seeking employment in three main ways:

(1) Blanket requirements attempting to ease the way into open employment, e.g. the Quota Scheme.

(2) Designated employment and the provision of special tools/aids/equipment for handicapped people in ordinary jobs, plus travel to work and alteration of buildings.

(3) Providing sheltered employment for those who cannot work in open employment. Recent legislation such as the Chronically Sick and Disabled Persons Act 1970 and the Chronically Sick and Disabled Persons (Amendment) Act 1976 has contributed to a growing climate of opinion which accepts that handicapped people have a right to work and gain access to places of employment.

Employers, too, are coming to realise that the handicapped can be good workers, and imaginative schemes are in hand to encourage them to make as many jobs as possible available to handicapped workers. Good examples of this are afforded by the Manpower Services Commission's 1979 'Fit to Work'

Campaign and BBC radio's publicity drive in the 1981 Year of the Disabled.

References

1. Brown, J.A. (1954) *The Social Psychology of Industry* (Harmondsworth: Penguin Books)
2. The Open University (1975) *The Handicapped Person in the Community*, Course P. 251 Unit 12, para 1:1, p. 12 (Milton Keynes: Open University Press)
3. Department of Education and Science (1978) *Special Educational Needs. Report of the Committee of Enquiry into the Education of Handicapped Children and Young People* (The Warnock Report), Cmnd 7212, p. 41 (London: HMSO)
4. Thomas, E. and Ferguson, T. (1964) *The Handicapped School-leaver* (London: British Council for Rehabilitation of the Disabled)
5. Tuckey, L., Parfitt, J. and Tuckey, B. (1973) *Handicapped School-leavers: Their Further Education, Training and Employment* (Windsor: National Foundation for Educational Research (NFER))
6. The Warnock Report (1978) p. 391
7. Pringle, M.L.K., Butler, N.R. and Davie, R. (1966) *11,000 Seven-Year-Olds* (London: Longman)
8. The Warnock Report (1978) p. 164
9. Andrews, R.J. (1976) 'Vocational Training Programmes for the Handicapped in Transition from School to Work' in J. Elkins, F. and E. Schonell *From School to Work* (University of Queensland, Educational Research Centre)
10. Mattingley, S. (1977) 'Employment and Training Services' in S. Mattingley (ed.) *Rehabilitation Today* (London: Update Publications)
11. The Warnock Report (1978) p. 182
12. National Youth Employment Council (1974) *Unqualified, Untrained and Unemployed* (Working Party Report) (London: HMSO)
13. Manpower Services Commission (1977) *Young People at Work. Report on the Feasibility of a New Programme of Opportunities for Unemployed Young People* (The Holland Report) (London: HMSO)
14. The Warnock Report (1978) p. 191
15. Lowman, P. (1977) 'Further Education Colleges and the Young Handicapped Adult', unpublished paper presented at DES Course N 83, Froebel Institute, London, July

CHAPTER 2

Student Needs: The Implications for Course Design

When dealing with handicapped adolescents, individuality of educational programmes is central to curriculum planning; but without losing this concept, it is possible to identify certain general levels and avenues of approach. The first of a recent set of surveys was that of the National Council for Special Education in 1975.[1] This working party was concerned to examine the current situation regarding the opportunities for handicapped school-leavers in the areas of *further education*, *training*, *employment* and *leisure pursuits*, and to make recommendations. In the area that concerns us here (further education), the survey asked three main questions and, with an over-all response rate of 82 per cent, obtained the following replies.

(1) *Have you any special courses for handicapped young people in your LEA/
    College?*
    A. Full-time courses for handicapped
        school-leavers of one year or more   — *15 Colleges*
    B. Full-time courses for handicapped
        school-leavers of up to one year   — *9 Colleges*
    C. Part-time courses (the type of course offered in this category varied
        almost in direct proportion to the number of colleges replying to the
        questionnaire, but the analysis revealed a number of trends):
        (i) Remedial literacy/numeracy   — *21 Colleges*
        (ii) Cookery, pottery and allied courses   — *10 Colleges*
        (In all, 60 course lines were available under this heading)
    D. Link courses – linked school/college   — *35 Colleges*
    Link courses again varied in direct proportion to the number of colleges
    offering them. However, a majority of courses were in one of two
    categories:
        (i) Vocational or semi-vocational area, e.g. engineering, business
            studies, catering, etc.
        (ii) Recreational/social classes, e.g. typing, fashion and dress,
            cookery, etc.
        The majority of students attended college for one full day per week but
        the range was from half day blocks to three full days.
    E. Courses in specialist colleges   — *28 Colleges*
        Whilst not all the above described themselves as colleges of further

education, they did claim to be making educational provision available for post-16 handicapped young people. Twenty-two centres of this group were offering, principally, vocational training courses of national recognition requiring a fairly high degree of ability. Courses for the low ability group in the vocational field, including the ESN(S), were, however, available within this group.

(2) *Do you make provision in the ordinary courses for any category of handicap? Please specify.*

    A. Replies to this question were received from *77 Colleges* indicating that they were prepared to offer places to handicapped young people to a lesser or greater degree.

    B. *72 Colleges* indicated that every effort was made to accommodate handicapped students and made reference to adaptations which had been made. Most of this group stated explicitly that they could accommodate wheelchairs.

    C. *5 Colleges* indicated that they made limited provision in ordinary classes but, because of access problems, they could not accept wheelchair-bound students.

    D. *1 College* had prepared a handbook for disabled students.

    E. *3 Colleges* had arrangements with specialist colleges for the handicapped to accept handicapped students into their ordinary classes.

    F. Replies were received from some colleges stating that they made special provision for specific handicapped groups:

Handicap	*No. of colleges mentioning*
Epilepsy	4
Spastic	10
Physical handicap	41
Visual handicap	23
Deaf/partially hearing	15
Speech defects	1
Educationally deprived	1
ESN(M)	2
ESN(S)	3

(3) *Do you second staff to perform duties for the handicapped outside your FE College(s), e.g. in adult training centres for the mentally handicapped?*
In all, *24 Colleges* indicated that they seconded staff to perform duties for the handicapped in a wide variety of establishments outside the further education college, e.g. adult training centres, day centres, hospitals for the mentally handicapped, psychiatric hospitals, etc. The courses offered were equally varied but were mainly in the fields of basic education (literacy/numeracy) and social leisure pursuits.

(4) Replies were received from a further *65 Colleges* giving a negative answer

to all three questions, but many of these colleges clarified their position by stating that they were considering or intending to make provision for handicapped young people.

The overall picture of fragmentary and uneven provision pointed to the need for more specialist facilities for handicapped school-leavers in further education colleges and elsewhere.

Planning and Resources

Before any educational institution decides to admit handicapped students the implications need to be considered and an admissions policy devised. A most important aspect of planning is staff and student attitudes, which need to be positive if the exercise of involving handicapped students in further education is to be successful: hence full discussion at all levels is essential. In this way, possible misconceptions can be dispelled beforehand. Once agreed, the policy should be given the maximum amount of publicity, both inside and outside the college. Ideally, this information can be transmitted via the college prospectus.

Problems of access to a building and mobility within it are likely to be an immediate concern. The 1970 Chronically Sick and Disabled Persons Act requires that these facilities be provided in new buildings together with specially adapted toilets, adequate parking and other necessary facilities. But existing buildings need to be brought up to these minimum standards so that access is created to all central college facilities such as canteens, libraries and other places of work.

Many of the existing teaching aids can easily be adapted to meet the special needs of handicapped students; for example, overhead projectors, commonly used in colleges, can be a useful aid when dealing with deaf students. Additionally, aids specific to individual students may be required for study. Obviously, handicapped students applying for places have to make known their own needs, and while applications have to be judged on merit or a student's suitability for a course, it is also necessary for the college to determine whether it can meet a particular applicant's special needs or not. For this reason, the Warnock recommendation that 'every establishment of further education should designate a member of staff as responsible for the welfare of students with special needs in the college' is fully endorsed.[2] As well as the welfare role identified by Warnock, this designated person can be responsible for briefing other members of staff.

If the best use is to be made of post-16 education by handicapped young people, initial and in-service teacher training courses have to equip staff to cope with these new students. Ideally, all teachers in further education should be given some training and experience in teaching the handicapped and should have access to 'top-up' facilities, as increasing numbers of these young people with a wide range of different handicaps are opting for ordinary or modified courses, or for courses specially designed for them, as advocated by Warnock.[3] The next section discusses ways in which the curriculum can be adapted with this in mind.

The Curriculum

'Wherever possible, young people with special needs should be given the necessary support to enable them to attend ordinary courses of further education.'[4]

Whilst many handicapped young people have been able to follow traditional courses either at ordinary colleges or at specialist colleges for the handicapped, like Hereward College, Coventry, it is probably true to say that there has been an inequality of opportunity, often because many handicapped young people lack the basic educational qualifications required for course entry when they leave school. In the light of this, it may be necessary for colleges to provide foundation courses designed to bring students up to acceptable levels. We have found that some students (mainly those with physical handicaps) taking the Business Education Council's General Diploma in Business Studies, for example, still require a good deal of support from a personal tutor in such subjects as English and arithmetic. Additionally, 'in-fill' students like these require some support in other areas, for example learning aids, transport and personal care. However, although the amount of support required is high, the number of such students is low, since probably only 10 to 15 per cent of all handicapped school-leavers are capable of working at a level where the academic content of courses is unmodified. But it does mean that a *majority* of colleges of further education might be involved at this level (referred to in Chapter 3 as Level One, see Figure 3.1).

Modifying Traditional Courses

'Some establishments of further education should experiment with modified versions of ordinary further education courses for young people with special needs.'[5]

Provision of this kind would mean modifying the duration, presentation and content of existing courses, together with a more liberal interpretation of entrance requirements. However, the major aim would still be to obtain a recognised qualification acceptable in industry and commerce. Approximately 25 per cent of all handicapped school-leavers could benefit from courses at this level (referred to in Chapter 3 as Level Two, see Figure 3.2). The disability that best illustrates the value of this kind of provision is hearing handicap where many students have potential but lack basic educational standards and have communication problems. The service provided for hearing handicapped students in Nottinghamshire indicates two ways in which this level of course can be applied in further education. For example, at Basford Hall College of Further Education are located three peripatetic further education lecturers, all qualified teachers of the deaf, who provide a support service not only to hearing-handicapped students on full or part-time courses in the county, but also to the lecturers teaching them. Classes in communication skills, the provision of aids and liaison with home/social services/industry are all features of the service. The Work Orientation Unit at the North Nottinghamshire College of Further Education offers the same service to hearing-handicapped students, but within one college of further education. There is an additional facility in that hearing-handicapped students with intellectual, physical and other disabilities can be catered for.

A Practical Example

Figure 2.1 illustrates a typical course structure for a hearing-handicapped student on a modified further education course. The core module of the course is Basic Cookery for the Catering Industry (EMEU 706) which takes up 50 per cent of the time allocated to catering practice and all of the time allocated to catering theory. Since this course is intended for day-release students from the trade, the handicapped student's lack of work experience is compensated for by an extra period of practical work together with a full day's work placement. This latter course component is not confined to just one work situation and the student is provided with a range of experience over periods of up to six weeks. Possible poor attainment in basic subjects is compensated for by a course component in this area, which can range from improving literacy and numeracy to gaining examination qualifications for the more able.

Many handicapped school-leavers lack social experience, partly because of the restrictive environment of special schools; those with hearing impairments being particularly vulnerable in this way. Social education programmes ranging from mobility and self-care on the one hand, to civics and citizens' rights on the other, have therefore been provided. All students in the Work Orientation Unit are encouraged to make the best of their leisure time, and the recreational course component offers a range of experiences, including physical activities, creative arts and practical skills. Throughout the course, support is provided by a specialist teacher of the deaf who is available to undertake remedial work in both the vocational area and basic education via the allocated tutorial sessions,

Figure 2.1: A Model Course Structure for a Hearing-handicapped Student

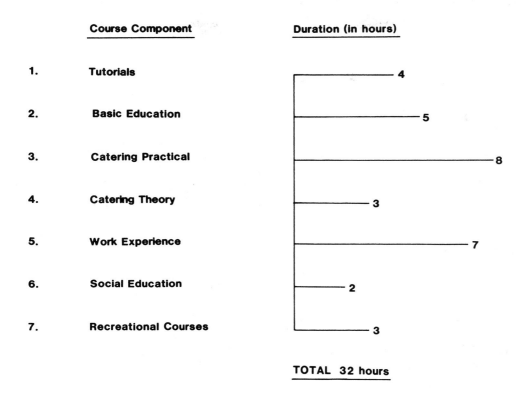

and also to give practical help and advice to other lecturers involved with the student. The use of induction loop hearing equipment and video-recording facilities have proved valuable, particularly in the practical sessions. Normally the course takes the student up to C2 level over two academic years. With most handicapped students, because of the extra time allocated during the weekly programme, the same course duration operates.

The National Study Group of Further/Higher Education for the Hearing Impaired – made up principally of lecturers in the field – has compiled a directory of courses which are being followed by hearing-impaired students. This, together with regular meetings, has helped tutors of the deaf and lecturers in further education to discuss the problems encountered by hearing-impaired students on various courses. In particular, the directory deals with aspects of tutorial support, course content and examination difficulties. For students on both ordinary and modified courses the question of examination difficulties arises from time to time. The National Bureau for Handicapped Students[6] believes that 'the purpose of any special arrangement should be to compensate for the restrictions imposed by handicap without impairing the validity of the examination'. In general terms, most examination bodies would accept this principle. However, there does seem to be the need for an acceptable code of practice to be worked out for the general guidance of both examination bodies and students.

Special Needs

'Some establishments of further education should provide special vocational courses at operative level for students with special needs and special courses of training in social competence and independence.'

'Within each region there should be at least one special unit providing special courses for young people with more severe disabilities or difficulties whch would be based in an establishment of further education.'[7]

If the type of further education courses described in the previous sections cater for up to 35 to 40 per cent of the handicapped school-leaving population, then a much larger proportion (in excess of 60 per cent) will have special needs which cannot be met by traditional further education courses nor even modified courses. It is not suggested that all such young people would benefit from further education, but the evidence shows that many more in this group are finding their way into colleges after leaving school, a move perhaps accelerated by general youth unemployment. It is not clear at the moment that colleges are providing them with anything very distinctive, anything very different from the schools they have just left. Traditional vocational courses in further education have fairly well-defined objectives usually leading to an examination qualification. Courses for the handicapped are not so self-evident and require not merely different course content and methods of teaching, but a fresh look at the whole curriculum in a vocational, educational and social context.

Green and McGinty (1979)[8] suggest three factors which need to be taken into account when designing the curriculum:

the student – his needs, aspirations and potential;
the teacher; and
the culture (specific areas of which are translated into subjects for teaching).

Obviously, the teacher must know his subject and have a clear understanding of the needs of his students but, more importantly, the teacher must also know something of the learning processes at work in his students. Green and McGinty list these as:

(1) Learning takes place at a slower rate and more opportunities for practice will be required.
(2) Verbal learning provides difficulties, and opportunities for practical experi-

ence will give meaning.

(3) Whilst the students may be aged 16 to 19, they may well be functioning at the level of 'concrete operations' in Piagetian terms (mental age 7-11 years) or well below the level of abstract thought.

(4) There are deficiencies in spontaneous learning which can be overcome by giving structure and direction to the learning.

(5) Transfer of learning and generalisation may be limited and there will be a need to practise new skills in a range of different situations.

(6) Interest and motivation levels may be difficult to maintain; this can be overcome by providing learning situations which give immediate reinforcement, are relevant and give direct experience.

(7) Teaching, by use of familiar situations, self-direction and other methods of independent working, should aim to enhance levels of self-confidence.

(8) The teacher will need to recognise that many students may be multi-handicapped and that problems in the learning situation may have more than one cause.

Since any or all of these limitations may apply to a particular student, programmes of work have to be organised on an individual basis. It is this feature in the education of the more severely handicapped which causes greatest difficulty for further education colleges, with their strong tradition of a *course-*based approach. An *individually* oriented curriculum means that the objectives set have to be relevant to the needs of the young people for whom they are intended. Every student lives in the world according to the way that he perceives it. The teacher has to remember that the student's perceptions may be different from his own, which means a starting off point for the curriculum at a level in keeping with the student's attainments, perceptions and interests (which may well be out of phase with his chronological age; see (3) above). Learning experiences should also form part of a planned development going right across the curriculum, not an *ad hoc* fragmented approach in each subject area.

In curriculum terms, a familiar problem with handicapped young people is that they have unrealistic aspirations and expectations which have to be reconciled with the facts of life in the real world. This can be done by gradually widening the young person's experience, which has often been too narrow for him to form judgements; if this process is managed carefully his perceptions will become more appropriate without his becoming discouraged. Students should always be presented with realistic and achievable goals, at the same time remembering that *too* easily attainable objectives can lead to a lack of motivation, and will have little value in the students' eyes.

Finally, *evaluation*: the clearer the *objectives*, the easier it is to evaluate, and thus modify, the curriculum via the objectives. If the teacher is clear exactly what he expects his students to be able to do, in observable and measurable terms, by the end of the course, then he will find it easier to evaluate and refine the curriculum as he goes along, and it will provide a frame of reference within which to work and be 'creative' within certain limits. He can then assess the effectiveness of his teaching by how closely it has achieved its stated objectives.

Having discussed the general approach to the curriculum required for the design of new courses for the more severely handicapped, we can now examine some specific work areas which will be followed up by practical examples in Chapter 3, where specially designed courses are referred to as Level Three courses (see Figure 3.3). Whilst the emphasis here will be on preparation for those who will be able to work in the traditional sense, the needs of those who cannot hope to do so will also be discussed in the final section.

Vocational Assessment and Guidance

For those who are severely handicapped, much care and skill is required if the assessment process is not to degenerate into a list of negative features detailing what an individual person cannot do (together perhaps with statements of opinion as to what he *should* not do). Warnock[9] gives four main criteria for effective assessment which may be summarised as follows:

(1) Parents should be closely involved and contribute to the assessment.
(2) It should aim to discover responses over a period of time and in a variety of settings and not be limited to performance on a single occasion.
(3) A wide range of professional expertise will be needed if full and appropriate assessment is to be carried out.
(4) Family and environmental circumstances as a whole will need to be incorporated into the assessment procedures.

The value of so-called 'short assessments' which appear to be both diagnostic and prescriptive upon the basis of a few days' experience with an individual is very doubtful. Appropriate assessment should call upon a range of expertise, information and opinion and should not be considered the prerogative of one particular individual or agency. The careers service, the school, psychologists, medical officers, social workers, the handicapped young person and his family will each have their individual contribution to make. Warnock[10] further suggests that, wherever possible, vocational assessment should take place on a local basis. For example, it is important that the needs and requirements of the local employment market are considered if employment for the student is a possibility. Above all, handicapped young people need to be assessed at two levels which recognise the fact that the ability to do a job, often involving knowledge and skills, is not necessarily synonymous with the ability to hold down that job. These two levels could be defined as:

(a) the *necessary* skills for work, as measured in the form of specific work skills either through test situations or, preferably, via practical working experiences; and

(b) the *sufficient* skills for work, in which an attempt is made to assess the individual's work personality, indicating his strengths and weaknesses as a worker. This assessment can only be achieved through continuing evaluation in a variety of situations during his training and work experience. In this way it will be possible to construct a personal profile of each student and to note progressive change.

Throughout the assessment process the objectives should be to establish base-lines of performance on which to build, and to recognise potential for further development. The profile of abilities and performance of a student can then be used as a check to ensure that the objectives set in the planning of his work programme are effectively evaluated, and also as the basis of a report to a potential employer.

Operative Level Vocational Courses

A college of further education can provide a foundation for vocational education for the more severely handicapped young person. However, this will require creativity and innovation on the part of college staff if handicapped students are not to be offered 'watered down' versions of traditional courses. Warnock[11] recommends 'special vocational courses at operative level for students with special needs'. An attempt to define operative level vocational education is not without its problems and complexities. In the past, many handicapped young people in this group have left school to go into routine work, or have been considered unsuitable for work, without any real regard to their latent potential. A reduction in demand for semi-skilled and unskilled labour has led to a decline in the number of handicapped young people going straight from school into work, and yet, at the same time, there is an increasing trend for the more severely handicapped to move into employment, as pointed out earlier.

The major criterion for the development of operative training/education must be that it is based firmly on the needs of the individual and the needs of industry within the young person's locality. Its principal aims should be:

(a) to sharpen the young person's industrial competence by introducing him to industrial skills, materials and practices; and

(b) to increase the young person's occupational adaptability, in particular to give him the social skills appropriate to the work culture.

These broad aims can be translated into individual programmes of work, which might include any or all of the following components:

specialised operative training workshops;
sample vocational courses;
limited skills training courses;
work experience programmes.

These will be discussed in more detail in Chapter 3.

Life and Social Skills

In discussing life and social skills, we shall use the definition of this term as provided by the Manpower Services Commission,[12] and illustrated in Figure 2.2. Within this very broad framework, there are three main areas which will require particular attention in so far as the more severely handicapped are concerned.

Basic Educational Skills

Many handicapped young people have experienced several years of teaching in literacy and numeracy, often with little apparent success. Further education courses which concentrate solely and exclusively on this area are not doing the best by the young people on the course if all they do is offer the same educational diet, the same practices and methods, in environments which are sometimes less favourable than at school. This is not to deny that basic education has a role in the provision of an appropriate further education curriculum for handicapped young people; but the new environment and culture of a college can change the motivational basis from an extrinsic situation to an intrinsic one, provided that the courses are based upon reality and first-hand experiences – for example, within the broad framework of the vocational programme, which will give both significance and purpose. This *adult* perspective can be enhanced by encouraging students to use public facilities such as libraries and classes available within adult education and literacy programmes. In this way, basic education can play a role in the support of vocational and social development programmes and at the same time improve the students' general standard of literacy and numeracy.

Social Skills

To those who are familiar with the problems of handicapped young people, the need for self-development is very obvious. Many special schools, even day

Figure 2.2: A Flow Chart of Social and Life Skills

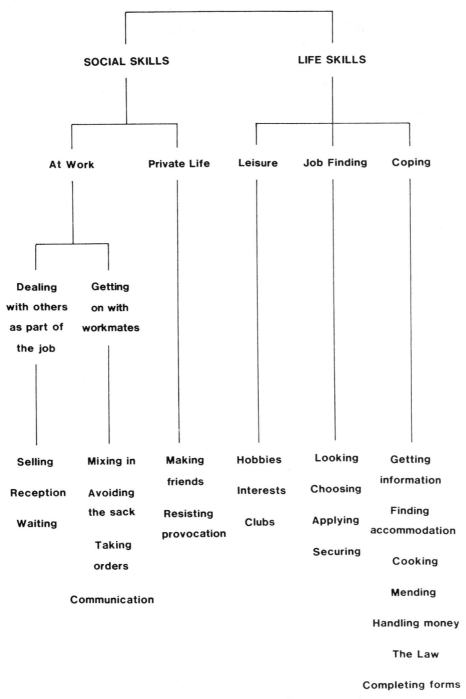

Source: Manpower Services Commission, 1977.

schools in large urban areas, are still physically and psychologically isolated, despite the efforts of some teachers. A limited range of educational experiences is often matched by low expectations on the part of staff, parents and, indeed, the young people themselves. There is often little social contact outside the range of those who are prepared to make allowances because of the individual's handicap. It is not surprising, then, to find that many handicapped young people coming into further education colleges, even those who are more capable academically, possess characteristics of immaturity and dependency, finding the new situation both confusing and threatening.

It is necessary, therefore, to devise individual programmes of short social skills courses in such areas as personal hygiene and grooming, health education, homecraft and personal relationships, together with more general areas like the use of public transport, communication systems, the welfare state and the responsibilities and benefits of membership of the wider community. In discussing assessment above, reference was made to the 'necessary' and 'sufficient' skills for work. Many handicapped young people either fail to obtain work, or having found a job soon lose it, because they are deficient in the area of 'sufficient' skills. Thus, an important aspect of a social skills programme is to ensure that a young person's social ability is in no way a hindrance to his vocational potential. As with all courses, it is not enough to subject a student to a varied range of social skills experience in the vague hope that he will benefit by them. Careful planning and structuring of courses is essential, and progressive evaluation, based upon noted behaviour change, will feed back into the system and allow for future planning.

Recreational and Leisure Skills

In the Report of the Working Party on Handicapped School-leavers of the National Council for Special Education[13] reference is made to the fourth area of study that the Working Party were concerned with, namely the leisure time facilities available to the handicapped. Whilst some 40 organisations responded stating that provision was made for the handicapped in leisure time pursuits (to which list could be added the facilities made available via local authorities, usually under the aegis of the Social Services Department), the general conclusions, summarised below, were not encouraging.

(1) Of the 40 organisations responding, many catered for school-age children, but very few made provision for young people once they had left school.
(2) Those bodies catering specifically for the handicapped recorded increasing memberships. Those primarily designed for the able-bodied recorded a lack of applications from the handicapped.
(3) There was great regional variation, with no facilities apparent in some areas. Facilities in London were the most favourable, these often being of the small self-help variety.

(4) The physically handicapped appeared slightly better off in terms of the number of organisations specifically dealing with them. There was, of course, evidence of considerable overlap of areas of disability catered for in all organisations. Of significance is the evidence suggesting that where physically and mentally handicapped young people were grouped together in clubs, the physically handicapped members tended to leave during their mid-teens.

(5) The main problems of providing facilities were (in descending order):
inadequate transport
access difficulties (for both participants and spectators)
lack of advice
lack of regular opportunities to participate in any type of activity on an integrated or specialist basis
general lack of funds
lack of applications from the handicapped to able-bodied organisations
poor liaison between clubs, schools and local authorities
lack of opportunity for the handicapped to be teachers in any activity
lack of accommodation
lack of voluntary helpers.

In general, the Report concluded that 'provision of leisure facilities for the handicapped school-leaver appears to be sporadic, unco-ordinated, under-funded by central and local government and far too dependent upon the individual goodwill of a small number of voluntary helpers'.

These conclusions are to be viewed with concern, especially as the amount of time available for leisure is likely to increase (though it has traditionally been high amongst the handicapped), and there is little evidence to suggest that facilities have improved since the Report was published in 1975. A placement in a college of further education, therefore, offers a handicapped young person access to a range of facilities for sport and exercise, expressive and creative arts and other recreational interest groups. It would appear that many do in fact take part in mainstream college activities and do not confine themselves solely to those for the handicapped. However, a problem arises when a young person leaves college and wishes to continue with a recreational interest. For this reason, at the North Nottinghamshire College, for example, handicapped students are encouraged to become involved in mainstream college activities but are also introduced to facilities available in their own areas through a recreational placement scheme begun in 1979. First of all, the leisure interests of the student are established by discussion, counselling or involvement in college activities. Then the lecturer responsible for the scheme checks the availability of facilities in the student's home locality and is able to introduce the student to them having first resolved problems such as transport, access and, possibly in some cases, parental opposition. Regular 'maintenance visits' are made by the lecturer to deal with any subsequent problems. In the normal course of events, students are introduced to a variety of experiences which include those specifically for the handicapped as well as mainstream activities. In the first six months of the scheme's operation, it has proved possible to place 50 per cent more students than had previously attended a college-based youth club.

Significant Living Without Work

We must accept that there are some handicapped young people who are unable to work and, whilst the main emphasis of this book is on preparation for work, the needs of this group must also be discussed, since many of them will receive further education. Attention was drawn to this particular area of concern by Warnock,[14] and although no specific recommendations were made, the benefits of working alongside others in a social context were referred to. There is an increasing number of handicapped young people with very limited, or no, potential for employment, combined with severe multi-handicaps who, perhaps, have an active mind imprisoned in a severely handicapped body, whose prospects are very limited and for whom the future holds nothing except total dependence on others.

When such young people are at school, the general aims of education are clear enough – namely that the opportunities and experiences for learning which are provided should aim at promoting their maximum development in all aspects of physical and psychological functioning. But it is as these very handicapped children grow older and leave school that uncertainties arise. Younghusband *et al.*, (1970)[15] suggest that: 'In the end there are two criteria by which successful adaptations to handicap are judged in adult life: the ability to earn a living and the ability to lead an independent life.' The implications of this statement have scarcely been regarded for the intelligent, yet unemployable, physically handicapped young person, let alone the retarded and multiply-handicapped. It is, however, a question that will have to be faced in the near future on an increasing scale and, in considering the problems, we shall be forced away from notions traditionally inherent in the terms 'education', 'school' and 'college'. A somewhat different concept of education will have to be developed, not limited to the attainment of intellectual and work skills, for it is even more important for these young people that the curriculum be strongly weighted towards life after leaving formal education, in particular towards personal independence, socialisation and recreational or creative fulfilment. These three themes would certainly yield the actual content of devised curricula, but a needs-based approach would be required and highly individualised programmes created. The themes which appear to be most urgent in terms of development are: (1) recreational/creative fulfilment; and (2) socialisation/independence.

For all handicapped students, education for leisure is almost as important as education for employment; but for those who are unable to work it is much more important. Hobbies, the arts, games and some forms of physical activities may well be within the young person's range of capability and, indeed, some like swimming and horse-riding can be of therapeutic value. Not only do recreational pursuits provide bridges to the able-bodied world but they also provide good opportunities to form relationships with peers, including the opposite sex.

One of the main dangers seems to be that the handicapped person at home too often establishes patterns of recreational behaviour that are passive, inward-looking and essentially unstimulating. The author's experience is that severely handicapped students spend a high percentage of time watching television or listening to a record player, and although these activites are reasonable enough in the proper context, it can be seen that they constitute a refuge in which the young person is often seen to be occupied, but in which the quality of interest and attention is such that only marginal enjoyment is obtained. It would be unreasonable to expect the home and family to undertake major upheaval and re-organisation solely to provide one handicapped member with adequate stimulation. Instead, it seems that the encouragement and fostering of recreational interests, especially practical skills and creative abilities, should be the responsibility of specialist agencies in both the statutory and voluntary sectors, with a view towards recreational skills being exercised not solely at home but also, and more appropriately, with other people in as wide a variety of settings as possible.

Many factors militate against the prospects of personal independence and social development in a handicapped young person living at home without employment. He may not be able to participate fully in family life; because of restrictions on mobility, visits to the cinema, pub, clubs and other places of entertainment with other young people are rare. A handicap further restricts the ability to initiate one's own recreation. The young person has few, if any, close friends, and as parents grow older and brothers and sisters leave home, the opportunities for shared recreation become less and less, with the result that those activities in which he does involve himself tend to be of a solitary nature and provide little contact with the wider world. Given more scope, however, the leisure time of handicapped young people could become abundantly more satisfying to them in terms of both social development and increasing personal independence.

The recreational placement scheme mentioned above has provided appropriate opportunities for social integration and the enjoyable use of leisure for those unable to work. Close liaison has to be maintained between Unit staff and other involved agencies, perhaps the most critical area being the establishment of an effective working relationship with parents. This is much more than a mere 'educational' relationship and calls for a collaborative partnership in respect of aims and objectives for the young person.

Appendix 2 gives details of a course for the severely handicapped, developed at the North Nottinghamshire College for Further Education since 1978–79. The initial reactions to this from the participants were good, and where changes were needed in the pilot year, they were able to suggest amendments.

An important feature of the course is that it attempts to prepare the students for their eventual placement outside the college. To end the course abruptly is both unnecessary and undesirable and, since the course content is specifically aimed at preparation for life in the community, the co-operation maintained between the Unit and the agencies outside concerned with this group is very important. So once a student leaves the college and is placed in a day centre, for example, he will be aware of and be able to participate in such other community provision as may exist which interests him.

This sharing of resources and expertise, though tentative at this stage, could become a future model to be adopted by further education and social services to the real benefit of the handicapped members of the community of all ages.

References

1. National Council for Special Education (1975) *Report of the Working Party on Handicapped School-leavers* (Stratford-upon-Avon: National Council for Special Education)
2. Department of Education and Science (1978) *Special Educational Needs. Report of the Committee of Enquiry into the Education of Handicapped Children and Young People* (The Warnock Report), Cmnd 7212, p. 175 (London: HMSO)
3. The Warnock Report (1978) pp. 210-11
4. The Warnock Report (1978) p. 174
5. The Warnock Report (1978) p. 174
6. National Bureau for Handicapped Students (1977) *An Educational Policy for Handicapped People* (London: National Bureau for Handicapped Students)
7. The Warnock Report (1978) pp. 174-5
8. Green, F. and McGinty, J. (1979) 'The Curriculum – Its Importance and Implications' in K. Dixon and D. Hutchinson (eds) *Further Education for Handicapped Students* (Bolton: Bolton College of Education (Technical))
9. The Warnock Report (1978) p. 59
10. The Warnock Report (1978) p. 165
11. The Warnock Report (1978) p. 174
12. Manpower Services Commission (1977) *Instructional Guide to Social and Life Skills* (London: HMSO)
13. National Council for Special Education (1975) *Report of the Working Party on Handicapped School-leavers*, pp. 23-8 (Stratford-upon-Avon: National Council for Special Education)
14. The Warnock Report (1978) pp. 202-3
15. Younghusband, E., Burchall, D., Davie, R. and Pringle, M.L.K. (eds) (1970) *Living with Handicap* (London: National Bureau for Co-operation in Child Care)

CHAPTER 3

Practical Applications

Much of the discussion of the practical applications of courses for handicapped young people in this chapter is based upon the author's experience in developing the Work Orientation Unit at the North Nottinghamshire College of Further Education since 1970. A brief decription of the Unit and the way it recruits its students is therefore appropriate at this stage.

Establishing a Work Orientation Unit

Provision for handicapped school-leavers began in 1969 on a pilot basis. There were two main factors in this development:

the personal experience of the College Principal in running link courses for ESN(M) pupils at another college;
the fact that the further education and training needs of handicapped students in the surrounding catchment area were not being catered for.

Following a successful pilot stage, the phased development of the project was planned on operational research lines with three main principles in mind:[1]

(1) To develop provision for all types of handicapped school-leavers.
(2) The integration of special education and technical education by:
(a) the recruitment of a staffing team from special education backgrounds. This team to be used in general education within a framework of further education; and
(b) the development and recruiting of staff teams from industrial and commercial backgrounds. These teams to be used for technological education and training within a framework of special education.
(3) The development of appropriate courses, accommodation and equipment.

Further principles in planning have subsequently emerged, following the growth in size of the Unit to full departmental status in 1972 (see Table 3.1). These were:

(4) The new (Work Orientation) department would be responsible for recruitment, welfare, work experience, basic literacy/numeracy, careers and social education.

(5) The present technical departments would provide the technological education and training.

(6) The technical teaching staff involved in the work for the handicapped would also be involved with normal students in order to remain open to essential influences, e.g. from the environment of industry and commerce, technical education and training.

Table 3.1: Development of the Work Orientation Unit (North Nottinghamshire College of Further Education) 1969-78

Year	Students	Teaching Staff	
		Special	Technical
1969	4	—	3
1970	10	1	3
1971	43	4	12
1972[a]	85	7	20
1973	85	8	20
1974	111	10	25
1975	117	11	30
1976	132	11	35
1977	159	12	35
1978	147	13	33

Note: [a] Indicates the formation of the Work Orientation Unit as a separate department from the staff with special education backgrounds.

The requirement of the special education staff was designed so as to create a pool of experienced and qualified staff in the areas of physical, intellectual, emotional and sensory handicap. The recruitment of the technical teaching staff was on a voluntary basis from interested staff who were given appropriate in-service training, initially on an internally designed programme, but currently using the City and Guilds 731 Certificate course *Teaching of the Handicapped in Further Education*, introduced for the first time in 1977.

In addition to the integrated approach developed within the College, there has been a great deal of involvement with outside agencies as indicated in Table 3.2. The role of these agencies and the support they can give will be discussed in Chapter 4.

Currently, the Work Orientation Unit provides further education facilities for handicapped young people within a catchment area which covers Nottinghamshire, parts of Derbyshire, South Yorkshire, Lincolnshire and, occasionally, elsewhere in the United Kingdom. The range of handicaps provided for is illustrated by the 1978–79 enrolment figures (total 147):

43 students with physical handicaps (e.g. Spina Bifida, Cerebral Palsy, head

injury, etc.);
71 students with intellectual handicaps (ESN(M) and (S)):
15 students with emotional handicaps; and
18 students with sensory handicaps (blind/partially sighted, deaf/partially hearing).

A list of this kind does not indicate the numbers of students who are multiply-handicapped or who possess conditions such as epilepsy and language disorders.

Table 3.2: Major Parties Involved in the Work Orientation Unit

(1)	Further Education Service	Central LEA and local
(2)	College	Principal, vice-principal, college-counsellor, technicians, Departments of Community Studies, Building, Engineering, Mining Engineering, Business and Management Studies, General Studies and Science
(3)	Careers Service	Central LEA and local
(4)	Medical Services	Area Health and local
(5)	Social Services	Central LEA, local and voluntary
(6)	Special Education	Central LEAs and schools within the catchment area
(7)	Department of Employment	Regional and local officers of TSD and ESD especially disablement resettlement officers
(8)	Department of Health and Social Security	National, regional and local
(9)	Parents	Individual and group contacts
(10)	Industry/Commerce/Trade Unions	through work contracts, work experience and placements
(11)	Voluntary Organisations	e.g. Royal Association for Disability and Rehabilitation, Spastics Society
(12)	Professional Organisations	e.g. National Council for Special Education

In what follows, the themes outlined in Chapter 2 are taken up in more detail, using practices developed in the Unit as examples of practical application. Again the major emphasis is on work preparation for those who are more severely handicapped.

Referral

Candidates for entry to the Work Orientation Unit are referred mainly by the Careers Guidance Service of the Local Education Authorities concerned and strong links are maintained with this service for as long as a student remains in college. Occasionally, referrals come from other sources, as indicated in Table 3.3, but even in these cases an attempt is made to involve the Careers Service.

Table 3.3: Sources of Entry to the Work Orientation Unit

	%
Careers officer directed entry from school	70
Careers officer or disablement resettlement officer directed entry from work failure	15
Entry directed via Social Services, heads of schools and other educational establishments, adult training/day centres	10
Parental initiative	5

Ideally, a candidate's first interview with a careers officer should be at least eight to twelve months before entry to college in order that full discussions and consultations can take place between the prospective student and his parents, his school, and the college and the careers officer, together with any other agencies involved, e.g. Social Services. It has proved necessary to construct a rather complex application form with sections to be completed by the school, social worker, doctor and careers officer (see Appendix 3 for specimen pages). This is because we have found that a report completed by one agency may stress a particular point giving an unreasonable bias to the total picture. The choice of the careers officer as the 'named person', as defined by Warnock,[2] gives not only the young person a single point of contact, but provides for the college a single line of communication which makes it easier for individual contributions to be co-ordinated.

Placement on Courses

For all students, the basis of their assessment is the application form. For many this, together with their interview, is all that is required, following which they can be placed in a course appropriate to their abilities and interests; perhaps normal further education courses or modified versions, referred to earlier, which cover the broad areas of:

> engineering
> construction
> general studies and science
> business and management studies
> community studies (e.g. dress, needlework, fashion, art, home management and family care).

Figures 3.1 and 3.2 illustrate the pattern of provision on these courses, which are described as Level One and Level Two. Many students, initially, cannot aspire to courses at the first two levels, and for these students, who in the main are more severely handicapped, special courses (Level Three) have been designed.

Figure 3.1: The Pattern of Provision on Normal Further Education Courses —
Level One (1 to 2 years duration)

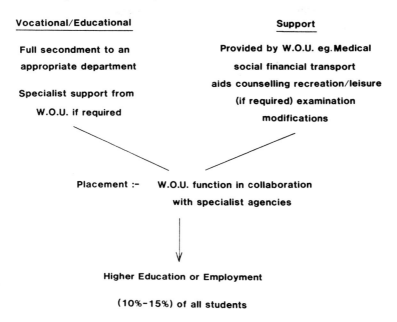

Vocational/Educational

Full secondment to an
appropriate department

Specialist support from
W.O.U. if required

Support

Provided by W.O.U. eg. Medical
social financial transport
aids counselling recreation/leisure
(if required) examination
modifications

Placement :-   W.O.U. function in collaboration
with specialist agencies

Higher Education or Employment

(10%-15%) of all students

Figure 3.2: The Pattern of Provision on Modified Further Education Courses —
Level Two (1 to 2 years duration but may involve return on a day release basis)

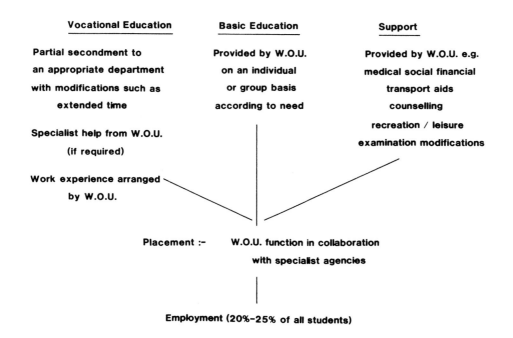

Vocational Education

Partial secondment to
an appropriate department
with modifications such as
extended time

Specialist help from W.O.U.
(if required)

Work experience arranged
by W.O.U.

Basic Education

Provided by W.O.U.
on an individual
or group basis
according to need

Support

Provided by W.O.U. e.g.
medical social financial
transport aids
counselling
recreation / leisure
examination modifications

Placement :-   W.O.U. function in collaboration
with specialist agencies

Employment (20%-25% of all students)

Figure 3.3: The Pattern of Provision on Specially Designed Courses — Level Three (2+ years duration)

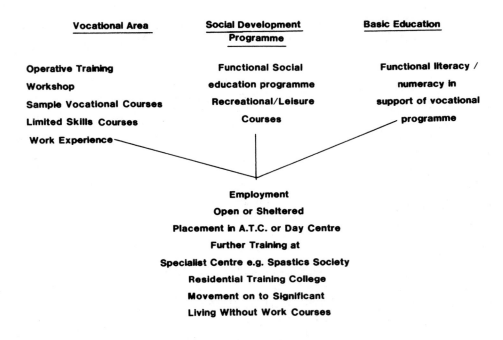

It is possible, however, for a student to 'move up' after having started at Level Three.

Level Three Courses

Because of the numbers of students and the complexity or severity of their disabilities, it is at Level Three that the majority of the provision of the Work Orientation Unit is made. The rest of this chapter will, therefore, be devoted to a description and discussion of this. The general outline of Level Three provision is shown in Figure 3.3. It can be seen that the programme is broken down into three specific, but highly-related areas. A major component is obviously the vocational area and, since social education and basic educational programmes are well documented elsewhere (see Appendix 9 for useful texts), I shall limit myself to this important area, on which very little has been written and where, I believe, the Work Orientation Unit has been highly innovative.

Assessment

All students entering the Work Orientation Unit at Level Three are regarded as potential employees, and the overall aim is to assess their strengths and weaknesses as workers in terms of 'necessary' and 'sufficient' skills as described in Chapter 2.

Initial Assessment on Entry. The aims of this aspect of the assessment programme are:

(1) to contribute to the evaluation of the student's capacity for training and employment;
(2) to contribute to the evaluation of the student's aspirations for training and employment;
(3) in the light of (1) and (2) to provide a reasonable basis for counselling and placement in training situations.

A strategy is deployed, approximating to that described by Rodger (1951)[3] in his Seven-Point Plan, which aims to discover inclinations and abilities, patterns of strengths and weaknesses, positive assets and definite limitations, together with the need for possible modifications to the working environment which, in turn, should point towards relevant job opportunities. This is as follows:

(a) Physical and medical capabilities (including the sensory area);
(b) Educational attainment;
(c) General intelligence level;
(d) Special abilities and aptitudes, e.g.

spatial relations	hand-tool dexterity
clerical aptitude	eye-hand co-ordination
mechanical engineering	finger dexterity

(e) Interests and vocational preferences;
(f) Personal qualities, e.g. disposition and temperament;
(g) Other relevant factors, e.g. family background/support.

Much of the relevant information required, particularly that of a biographical nature, can be obtained from a correctly completed Unit application form. However, where gaps and doubts exist, further steps can be taken. For example, for areas (a) and (g), an initial medical assessment is made by the college doctor and nurse, to which parents are invited. For areas (b) to (e), standardised tests can be used:

Neale Analysis of Reading Ability[4]	} for area (b)
Vernon Graded Arithmetic-Mathematics Test[5]	
Raven's Standard Progressive Matrices[6]	for area (c)

Differential Aptitudes Test, Space-Relations Sub-test[7]
ACER Short Clerical Test[8]
ACER Speed and Accuracy Test[9]
ACER Mechanical Reasoning Test[10]   } for area (d)
Bennett Hand-tool Dexterity Test[11]
Crawford Small Parts Dexterity Text (eye-hand dexterity)[12]
Purdue Pegboard (finger dexterity)[13]

The use of standardised tests, however, requires very careful consideration with regard to applicability, reliability and validity. It has been possible to construct norms for both handicapped and able-bodied populations, in the same age group, by using normal college craft students whose performance can reasonably be expected to indicate acceptable levels for open employment. Nevertheless, relatively little use is made of standardised tests in comparison with practical training situations, which will be described later.

To gather more information in area (e) – interests and vocational preferences – all students have a structured interview with the Unit's Industrial Liaison Officer, who is an ex-careers officer. In this context, a vocational interests questionnaire, such as the Crowley Occupational Interests Blank,[14] may be used, which is well suited to this level of student. Recently, however, the Personal-Occupational Satisfactions Guide devised by Hutchinson (1977) with Unit students in mind,[15] has proved very useful as a basis for discussion. This guide, based on the work by Daws (1965),[16] makes easier the analysis of individual needs in the following areas:

Section A – Material values
Section B – Status
Section C – Skills
Section D – Dominant values
Section E – Associated values
Section F – Perceptual values

Beyond the information given in the application form, no specific measures of personal qualities (area f) are attempted in the initial stages of assessment. In our experience, it has more relevance as part of the on-going evaluation plan. The time span involved in initial assessment is:

(1) A half-day for areas (a), (b) and (c) which, together with the application form and the interview, permits education and training to begin.
(2) It can be expected that a sufficient amount of information in areas (d) to (g) will be revealed by the end of the first month in college to enable re-assessment of initial placements to be made. All information is entered on a *Basic Student Record Form* which gives details of the student's disability, attainments, aptitudes and general adjustment.

On-going Evaluation. Once initial assessment procedures are complete and a student is placed on a course, an *Information to Staff Form* is circulated to the departments concerned, for the information and guidance of lecturers involved in teaching handicapped students. A more personal contact is subsequently made by the student's own personal tutor (from the Work Orientation Unit), who is responsible for introducing and monitoring the work of that student while in college. The continuous assessment of students on Level Three courses follows a programme with two basic components:

(1) *Educational/training development* which includes the development of skills, accuracy, speed and working relationships, etc., in all vocational training and work experience situations except the special Operative Training Workshop, which has a separate set of procedures to be described later (pp. 44–58). Additionally, note is taken of gains or losses in general educational attainment. A *Student Progress Record* is completed by all staff teaching Work Orientation Unit students, and handed to the student's personal tutor who enters the information on a *Termly Progress Record*. This is submitted to the Deputy Head of the Unit, as Director of Studies, for monthly appraisal and changes of course in consultation with the tutor and student. A check is also kept on his general educational attainment, especially in literacy and numeracy, and progress recorded.

(2) *Social development* in training situations, both in and out of college, is recorded, since the acquisition of work skills and appropriate work behaviour determines the ultimate eligibility of a student for employment. This is also noted on the Termly Progress Record, and a check-list of specific characteristics completed once a term and recorded on the Basic Student Record Form. A yearly check-list of practical social skills is completed at the end of each academic year (see Appendix 4).

The structured framework of the evaluation system allows a constant check to be kept on each student's progress, which in turn indicates the need for remedial work or for the revision of objectives. The key person in the system is the personal tutor who is thus briefed on all aspects of a student's work and development. The information gathered is also used to prepare case conference reports and the formal written report which is submitted to parents at half-yearly intervals. Throughout, the emphasis is on identifying the strengths that a student has and attempting to use these to overcome any areas of difficulty.

Work Areas

The main areas of vocational work in which Level Three students operate were indicated in Figure 3.3. Owing to the individuality of programmes, it is difficult to state the amount of time that students spend on vocational work. As a general guide, however, it would be true to say that no student would start a programme with less than 50 per cent of his time being devoted to vocational work. At the other end of the scale, the maximum amount of time that would be given to vocational work would not normally exceed 80 per cent.

The structure of the vocational programme is broken down into four main areas:

Operative Training Workshop;
sample vocational courses;
limited skills vocational courses;
work experience.

These four main components are not designed to be exclusively self-contained units and the degree of inter-relationship is high. Table 3.4 indicates how the components might be arranged for students at the beginning (Example 1), in the middle (Example 2) and at the end (Example 3) of what is, in most cases, a two year course, with the possibility of extension if this is required.

Table 3.4: Possible Arrangement of Vocational Work Areas

Example	Course Component	Duration (no. of days per week)
(1)	Operative Training Workshop	2
	Sample vocational courses	1
	Basic/social education/recreational courses	2
(2)	Operative Training Workshop	1
	Sample vocational courses	1
	Work experience (i.e. general placement)	1
	Basic/social education/recreational courses	2
(3)	Limited skills vocational course (including 1 day per week relevant work experience)	4
	Basic/social education/recreational courses	1

Operative Training Workshop

The Operative Training Workshop provides the basic building block of every Level Three student's vocational programme. The concept of training at this level indicates a real departure from traditional vocational training for the handicapped and is a good example of innovation on the part of the Work Orientation Unit. The workshop is housed in accommodation completed in 1978, and we were fortunate in that the College was able to consult with the architect and incorporate its ideas into the design, in particular the open-plan aspect of the floor area of the workshop which permits re-adjustment of work areas according to need (see Figure 3.4).

Figure 3.4: Plan of Operative Training Workshop

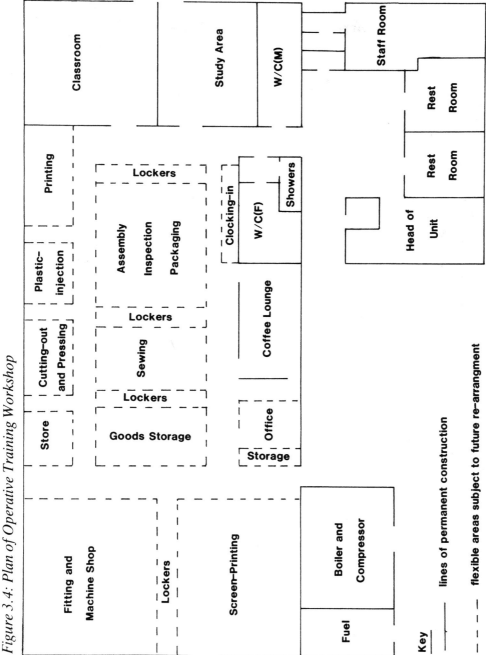

Classroom

Study Area

W/C(M)

Staff Room

Rest Room

Rest Room

Printing

Lockers

Clocking-in

Showers

Head of Unit

Plastic-injection

Assembly

Inspection

Packaging

W/C(F)

Cutting-out and Pressing

Lockers

Sewing

Coffee Lounge

Store

Lockers

Goods Storage

Office

Storage

Fitting and Machine Shop

Lockers

Screen-Printing

Boiler and Compressor

Fuel

Key

——— lines of permanent construction

– – – flexible areas subject to future re-arrangment

The purposes of the training workshop are threefold. It is used in the assessment procedure, described above, for all students at Level Three. Secondly, it is used for pre-training of students prior to vocational training proper. Finally, and most importantly, it is used for at least 40 per cent of all Level Three students, for training at an operative level prior to placement in open employment or referral to some other form of occupation, sheltered or otherwise. It is this latter function which occupies the majority of the workshop's facilities and what follows is primarily concerned with that. Based upon a diagnostic period in the workshop, it is possible to set training objectives for each student according to the model in Figure 3.5. At the end of the diagnostic period, together with initial assessment, information will have been obtained about the student's base-line situation. This information can be compared with what is accepted as general work behaviour. The difference between the base-line and acceptable level becomes the main focus of attention and it is necessary, at this stage, to write a programme of training objectives to suit the individual, in order that the discrepancy may be removed. Once the individual programme has been established, the student can be placed in various work situations that will benefit him. These work situations have been created by importing sub-contract work from industry, and also by developing direct college production lines. The main work areas cover:

engineering machining	printing
sewing machining	light assembly
fabric screen-printing	electronic wiring
plastic-injection moulding	inspection

together with such general workshop duties as storekeeping, delivery of goods and cleaning.

The task, or tasks, chosen for an individual student can be presented in the form of a task analysis sheet which:

(a) indicates the number of elements which make up the task;
(b) provides a brief description of each element;
(c) indicates the degree of control to perform each element.

An example of a task analysis sheet for one particular job can be found in Figure 3.6, where the task has been analysed as follows:

(a) The task has been broken down into its basic elements (or *therbligs*), each of which includes, where possible, the four basic movements of *reaching* for an object, *grasping* that object, *moving* it and *positioning* it (Column 2).
(b) The senses required to carry out each element are indicated (Column 3). These would normally include hearing, taste, sight, touch, smell, kinaesthetic.
(c) The degree of control required to perform each task (Column 4). In this

analysis the following descriptions of control are used:

1. simple movement 2. elementary control 3. moderate control
4. good control 5. fine control

In addition to control other activities involving perceptual processes might be analysed. These could include *planning*, *initiating*, *terminating* and *checking* a task.

The reduction of a task into its component elements also enables organisation of the workforce to take place. Figure 3.7, using the same example of the drill drift, illustrates this. Here, two groups of students, *X* and *Y* (five students in each group), are working. In *X*, four are of limited ability (*a b c d*) and

Figure 3.5: Model for Defining Specific Training Objectives

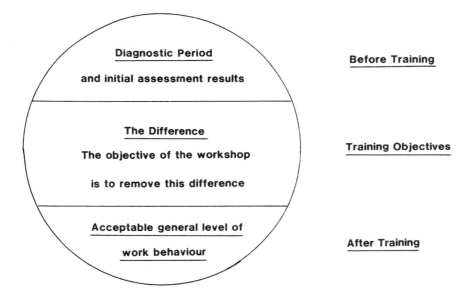

Figure 3.6: Task Analysis Sheet

Task: Removal of burrs on a drill-drift
Tools used: 6 inch flat smooth hand file

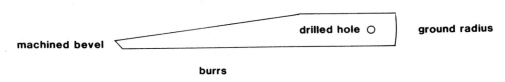

Element no.	Brief description	Sensory modalities involved	Degree of control
1	Select drift from box	V, T, K	1
2	Search machined edge on both sides for burrs	V, T	3
3	Hold drift at correct angle and file away burrs	V, T, K	3
4	Search machined bevel for burrs	V, T	3
5	Hold drift at correct angle and file away burrs	V, T, K	3
6	Search drilled hole on both sides for burrs	V, T	3
7	Hold drift at correct angle and file away burrs	V, T, K	3
8	Search ground radius on both sides for burrs	V, T	3
9	Hold drift at correct angle and file away burrs	V, T, K	3

Key: V = visual; T = tactile; K = kinaesthetic

consequently only perform a limited number of tasks, with the fifth (*e*) acting as an inspector. In *Y*, however, all five students are of equal ability and can perform all of the elements; the work is therefore organised so that each takes a turn at filing and inspecting on a rota basis.

Figure 3.7: An Example of Task Analysis/Work Force Organisation

Task   **Removal of burrs on drill drifts**

Example X	**No. of Workers = 5**	**Example Y**	**No. of Workers = 5**
Element No.	**Organisation of Work**	**Element No.**	**Organisation of Work**
1		1	
2	a	2	
3		3	a
4	b	4	b
5	e	5	c ⟷ e
6		6	d
7	c	7	
8	d	8	
9		9	

Whilst many students are only capable of limited degrees of control, some develop to do more difficult tasks requiring fine control. The photographs showing the stages in the assembly of a rotary electrical switch illustrate this.

Some tasks can be undertaken either solely by one person, or by a team, each doing a small part. Others cannot be done by a single person and the team approach must be used. This is illustrated by the photographs showing the stages in the manufacture of an electric fencing post, in which a metal spike has to be heat shrunk into a plastic tube. The stages here are:

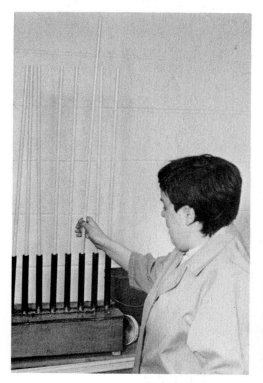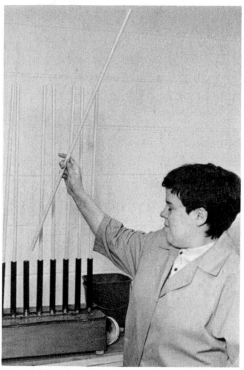

(a) heating the plastic tubes

(b) inserting the metal spikes

(c) inspecting and cleaning

(d) bundling into 50s

This sort of situation is useful in demonstrating to students the interdependence of one with the other in the production line approach.

The overall aim of the initial period of time spent in the Operative Training Workshop is to help students adjust to industrial life, not to train them for particular trades and crafts, though part of the process does inevitably involve being able to give a fairly accurate assessment of a student's aptitude and potential for work in a particular area, and this may well be followed up by specific training at a later stage. Many of the elements that make up 'general work behaviour' can be observed in the situations provided by the workshop, and moving the students through these as suggested in Figure 3.8. The three variables indicated here of *situation*, *number of elements* and *degree of control* have many variations which can be altered so as to create specific experiences for particular students. When a student is working on a particular task he is given a job card (see Appendix 5) which he is expected to use. This, together with the follow-up task sheet which would normally be completed by the student as part of his basic education work, brings both literacy and numeracy into the practical

(e) packing into 100s

work scheme.

One of the problems inherent in a simulated workshop is the reality-limitation of it not being paid employment. To try and obviate this, a rewards system, based upon individually determined goals for work performance measured in terms of output and behaviour, has been created. Credits are awarded to the students according to the goals set and these can be exchanged for a variety of goods, including some of the clothing made in the workshop. If levels of behaviour and performance are unacceptable, then negative credits can be awarded and are deducted from the total.

Figure 3.8: General Work Behaviour Experiences

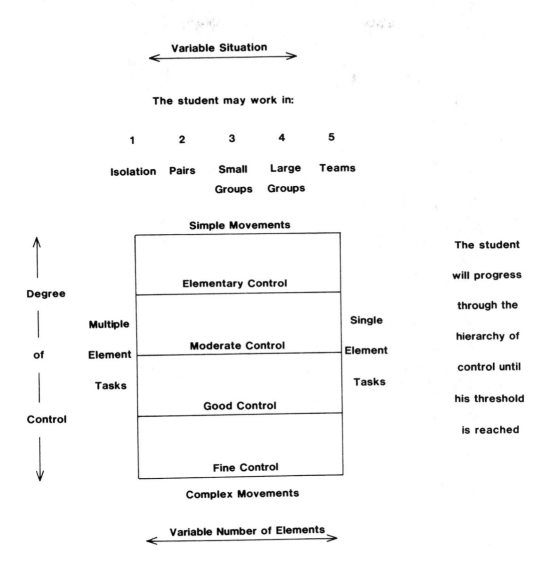

At this first stage of training, when emphasis is being placed on adjustment to work, it is necessary to ensure that the assessment procedures reflect this. To this end, a series of *lowest common denominators* in work behaviour have been identified and these are used irrespective of the type of work being undertaken. They are:

(1) *Punctuality* — this is easily monitored via the clocking-in and out system.
(2) *Relationship with peers* — this item is intended to cover general sociability with peers: whether a student causes annoyance to other students while working; whether he can converse at a social level but still carry on working; etc.
(3) *Relationship with staff* — this is the general attitude towards the authority figure in the work environment which can change from time to time.
(4) *Reaction to stress on different tasks* — covering such areas as reaction to directives to increase output and/or quality, and reaction to peers in task situations requiring co-operation.
(5) *Application to the task* — involving such things as the amount of effort required in order to get the student to work; whether application is limited to short periods only or is maintained throughout the working day.
(6) *Physical capacity to do the task* — aspects involved here would be whether physical disabilities prevent efficient work on certain tasks: such things as eyesight, strength, dexterity, co-ordination, mobility.
(7) *Acquisition of training* — involving the ease with which a task is learned, together with the amount of teaching required.
(8) *Accuracy* — this indicates the magnitude of error on certain tasks and is, in essence, a measure of the quality of work.
(9) *Speed* — to complement the item above, this indicates the quantitative side of work.
(10) *Ability to follow instructions* — covers day-to-day instructions concerning all areas of work in general and is to be distinguished from instructions given in learning tasks — see item (7).
(11) *Ability to communicate* — consists of the ability to communicate to staff and peers regarding the task being worked on.
(12) *Ability to withstand fatigue* — this is to indicate whether certain tasks demand so much of a person's attention and ability that they display signs of physical and mental fatigue.

At first these twelve areas of work behaviour were assessed weekly; however, it was soon found that this basis of time was insufficient to note any real movement or change and it was adjusted to a monthly basis, which now links in with the on-going evaluation indicated above. Visual records of monthly performance with termly summaries, together with information on the number of credits earned, are kept in the workshop for reference (see Figure 3.9), and a monthly report is given to the student's personal tutor for inclusion in his

Figure 3.9: Examples of Items on Profile Sheets (Workshop Reference)

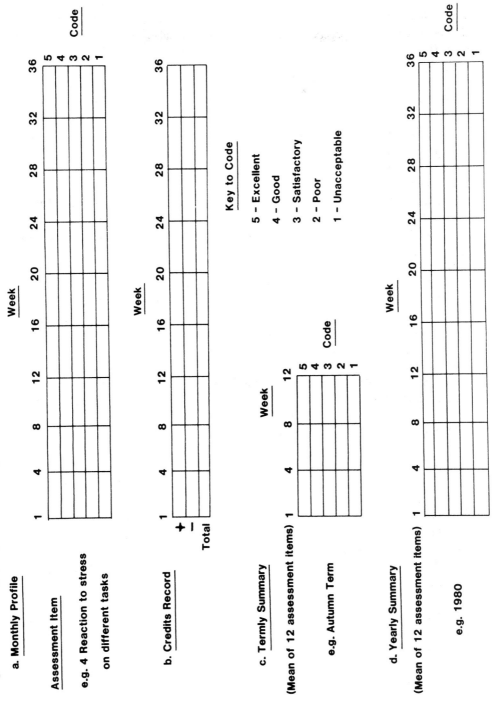

records. Records are also kept on the different tasks that a student undertakes, in order that comparisons can be made. This latter information is invaluable when counselling the student regarding his work aspirations and interests since, for many students, the opportunities provided by the Operative Training Workshop represent their first experience of a work situation. One of the main difficulties is creating an appropriate work environment. Many of the young people coming into the workshop for the first time have just left school and still see it as an extension of their previous experience and behave accordingly, Clearly, this is one of the reasons why the workshop was considered necessary in the first place. Without this experience those students with adjustment problems probably would not get work or would drift into a pattern of 'job-hopping', with increasing periods of unemployment in between. To try to resolve this area of difficulty, the work has been divided into three main areas (see Figure 3.10).

(a) *Basic work* — which involves all new students and requires a high level of staff supervision.

(b) *Semi-skilled work* — which involves all students at some time and alternates between high and low levels of staff supervision according to the nature of the work being undertaken.

(c) *Skilled and high responsibility work* — which will not involve all students but only those capable of working under minimum supervision.

Not all work areas fit neatly into the categories requiring high and low levels of supervision, but this general method of organisation does ensure that the maximum staff input is at the level where it is most required, i.e. in the initial stages of a student's time in the workshop, and allows for an increasing amount of student responsibility and independence as he progresses through the various stages of workshop experience. A period of full-time placement can be followed by other vocational courses or, more commonly, a student would spend a period of time in the workshop of usually two days a week (see Table 3.4) and not exceeding three, with the rest of the week being allocated to sample vocational courses, basic education, social education and recreational courses.

Obviously, the work undertaken in an innovative workshop such as this takes several years to develop, and while sub-contract work from industry provides some experience, the range is not comprehensive. If it were the only type of work to be undertaken, not only would training be limited, but there would be a real danger of production taking precedence over training. Direct college production would seem to be the answer and this aspect of the workshop has been planned to operate as a research and development project spreading over a number of years. It not only represents a new educational and training area for handicapped students, but also involves normal college students, so far including those from the departments of Business and Management Studies (BEC National Diploma, GCE 'A' level Accounts, Secretarial Studies); Community Studies (GCE 'A' level Art, 'A' level Dress, Home Economics and Fashion);

Figure 3.10: Areas of Work and Responsibility in the Operative Training Workshop

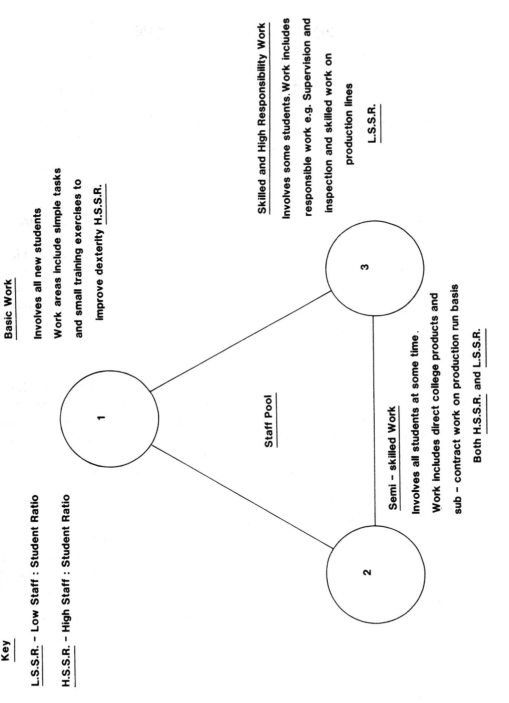

Key

L.S.S.R. - Low Staff : Student Ratio

H.S.S.R. - High Staff : Student Ratio

Basic Work

Involves all new students

Work areas include simple tasks
and small training exercises to
improve dexterity H.S.S.R.

Skilled and High Responsibility Work

Involves some students. Work includes
responsible work e.g. Supervision and
inspection and skilled work on
production lines

L.S.S.R.

Staff Pool

Semi – skilled Work

Involves all students at some time.
Work includes direct college products and
sub – contract work on production run basis
Both H.S.S.R. and L.S.S.R.

and Engineering (Craft and Technical level courses). The main areas which have been developed to date in this project are:

Fabrics (including clothing, soft furnishings, fabric painting, labelling and packaging);
Metal products (including soldering iron bits, wrought iron-work simple fabrication, milling and turning);
Plastic products (lobster pot rings, easy-joints, chess sets, draught pieces and skin-packaging).

Production is on a small batch basis with normal college students involved in design, setting-up, marketing and financial control, and with handicapped students being involved at the production level relevant to their training in motor skills, the associated cognitive learning, and work behaviour.

Sample Vocational Courses

Whereas the initial part of a student's vocational preparation spent in the Operative Training Workshop is not designed to offer specific training for particular areas of work, the purpose of sample vocational courses is to awaken the student to the possibility of working in a particular field and to help in assessing his capability for work in that field, a special feature of the process being the student's own appraisal of his potential and interest. Sample vocational courses are available in:

engineering	sewing-machining
brickwork	domestic cookery/trades
plumbing	hairdressing
painting/decorating	retail trades
carpentry/joinery	fabric printing/printing
horticulture/playing field maintenance	plastic moulding/packaging

with general work experience also being included.

These courses are operated either within the relevant college department or within specific areas of the training workshop on a half-day block basis, with regular changes in the cycle of experience provided according to the assessment of individual student progress.

It is difficult to specify the time which needs to be devoted to this combination of initial operative training and sample vocational work, but in the majority of cases students have established their levels of performance and areas of interest by the end of the first academic year and can move on to the next stage of training. Those students who cannot move on, because of lack of ability, are considered to have reached the maximum of their potential and will spend the next year in college consolidating their skills in the workshop and by being placed on work experience. It is likely that some within this group will be judged as unemployable and so referred, for example, to an adult training centre. Many of these 'unemployable' young people, however, could make a valuable contribution in a protected environment, although places in sheltered workshops and in enclave situations within open industry are unfortunately difficult to obtain.

Limited Skills Training Courses

An important area of innovation in the special course provision in further education for the handicapped lies in the development of limited skills training. Essentially, the aim of these courses is to provide operative level training and experience within a general vocational area and to develop any specific aptitudes recognised. Table 3.4 indicated that up to four days per week can be spent on this type of course, with the fifth day being used for other relevant courses. In the total planning of a limited skills course, work experience is provided for. However, the nature of the work experience may vary: on some courses it is organised on the basis of one day per week throughout the duration of the course (e.g. courses in retail and domestic trades), while on other courses a period of block release is organised towards the end (e.g. courses in engineering, building and sewing machining).

The duration of a limited skills course is usually 36 weeks (or one academic year), but this can be extended for a further period of 36 weeks if necessary. As a result of limited skills training, some students show such ability that they are able to move on to a Level Three course. This can be undertaken on a full-time basis, e.g. integrated basic training in mechanical engineering, electrical engineering and fabrication/welding; or the student can obtain employment and return to the college on a part-time day release basis with continued support from the Work Orientation Unit if required. Overall, limited skills courses provide practical training which should enable a student to gain employment of a semi-skilled nature in industry or commerce.

Limited skills training is available in the same areas as previously indicated for sample vocational courses. Full details of the General Operatives Building Course, organised with the Department of Building, are given in Appendix 6, and some idea of the courses in engineering and sewing-machining is given in the accompanying illustrations.

Formal assessment procedures for these courses are as described for on-going evaluation (p. 43), but an attempt is made to involve the student much more closely in the process. A useful way of doing this is via a training log-book which states the purpose and content of the course and in which the student can record details of his work and progress. This log-book is assessed as part of course work and can be presented to a prospective employer as valid documentation of the type of work undertaken and degree of success achieved. An example of a log-book for the Engineering Limited Skills Course is given in Appendix 7.

Engineering: Limited Skills

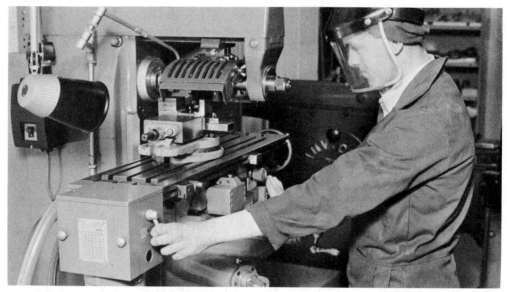

Horizontal milling

Shaping

Setting up centre lathe

Limited Skills Course in Sewing-machining

Lock-stitch sewing

Detail of industrial training sheet used in lock-stitch sewing

Over-locking on a production run

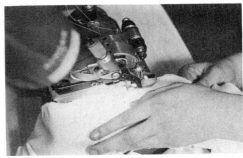

Detail of over-locking

Manufacture/covering of buttons

Detail of button covering

Work Experience

The final practical component of the vocational preparation at Level Three (and also at Level Two, as indicated in Chapter 2) is work experience. The general aim of this is to enable students in the Unit to participate in a period of industrial experience as part of their preparation for employment. Specific details of the scheme can be found in Appendix 8. The students taking part in work experience are those it is recommended for as part of on-going evaluation, and it appears at different levels:

(1) For Level Two students undertaking a specific course of vocational training available to normal students, but with modifications to compensate for the lack of industrial experience.
(2) As part of the widening horizons featured in sample vocational courses.
(3) To consolidate skills and learning for those students unable to progress to limited skills training.
(4) To give specific experience to those students on limited skills vocational courses.

Whether the work experience provided be specific or general, there is an obvious link with the student's social development since both practical and social experiences are required. Some students, though ready to practise vocational skills in a meaningful setting, are not capable of the adjustment required to undertake work experience out of college. For this reason, a number of *internal work experience* placements are available in college. These can involve working with the technical, clerical, caretaking or domestic staff, or it can mean being involved in a full-scale production run in the Operative Training Workshop. The accompanying illustration shows a student using an injection-moulding machine to produce a plastic lobster pot ring. In either case, the demands made of the student, in terms of length of working day and working conditions, are the same as for *external work experience*. Up to 80 students per week find themselves on work experience in a placement outside college and, unless there are exceptional reasons, this placement is made in the student's home locality. Placements range from one day per week regularly throughout the course, to a period of three to four weeks block release towards the end of the course. Wherever possible, attempts are made to change work placements at intervals in order to give the student a cycle of different experiences.

In both forms of work experience frequent contact is made with the employer and the student for assessment and follow-up purposes. It becomes very noticeable that after a relatively short time on placement the student becomes much more aware of the world of work and is able to measure up his own abilities (and limitations) against the standards required in industry. Additionally, the student's ideas tend to broaden and he makes wider social contacts which help him

to consolidate and give significance to the training and education given in college.

Work Induction and Placement

Whilst the majority of time devoted to vocational preparation is of a practical nature, there is obviously scope to undertake work, based in the classroom, of general applicability to all Level Three students. Work induction sessions, therefore, aim to give each student a wider knowledge of himself and the kind of employment within his home area; and attention is drawn to the various departments which will help with employment difficulties, for example, the Careers Service, the Disablement Resettlement Service and Social Services. The programme is usually a one-hour weekly session based upon group discussion and participation, film, radio and TV material, practical projects, visiting speakers, role-playing exercises and visits to places of employment, together with the practical experiences that the student has gained both in and out of college. A work induction notebook is kept by each student and this is used to record and collate information gained during the course for future use. Specific areas of work covered include: *self-analysis projects*, in which the student is encouraged to get to know himself better in terms of strengths and weaknesses, likes and dislikes and attitudes; and *job-analysis projects*, where the student looks at the working environment in terms of what is available in his own area, what the immediate members of his family and friends do, individual firms and jobs. Using these two areas, a matching exercise can then take place where the student looks at the information gained on his interests, on job requirements and job satisfactions and begins to see where his future may lie. Information gained from initial assessment (e.g. the Crowley Occupational Interests Blank[14] and the Personal-Occupational Satisfactions Guide[15]) can provide a structured framework for a work induction programme. The student also has to acquire knowledge of the paraphernalia of documentation associated with work, and practical exercises are undertaken on application forms, insurance, income tax, wages and sickness benefits. Particular importance is paid to the procedures of finding, keeping, losing and changing a job, and of great value here is the involvement of the Careers Service, whose role will be discussed in the next chapter.

Placement of students from Level Three courses provides an increasingly difficult task at a time of economic recession, since the number of employment outlets is decreasing at the same time as the number of people seeking employment is increasing. Placement is generally decided in two stages. At the end of the first year of a course a review case conference is held to determine a student's programme for the subsequent year; then six months before he leaves the college there is a final conference to determine the ultimate area of placement. At both case conferences, the student and his parents attend and, in addition to the college staff, the careers service and other support agencies involved with the particular student are represented. The Unit has one member of staff designated to follow up conference decisions with the placement agencies. With the increasing difficulty of obtaining jobs and the resultant pressure on other areas of placement, it is important that sufficient time is given to this area, which is the culmination of the student's course and upon which so many hopes are placed. As indicated earlier, not every Level Three student is proved capable of undertaking open employment. Table 3.5 indicates the main areas of placement available and suggests trends accountable directly to the problems referred to above.

Table 3.5: Placement of Level Three Students from the Work Orientation Unit, North Nottinghamshire College of Further Education

Year	No. of students to be placed	Placement Area				
		Open employ-ment	Sheltered employ-ment e.g. Remploy	Adult training centre	Further training e.g. YOPs, training workshop	Not placed
1977-78	44	31	8	2	—	3
1978-79	75	26	6	10	16[a]	17[b]

Notes: [a] This facility first became available in the area in 1978-79. Follow-up studies have shown that following this placement, a final placement in open employment occurs in the majority of cases.

[b] This figure (22.5 per cent) is higher than usual (7 to 8 per cent for the previous three years) and includes those who are unemployable and not placeable in other provision, those who married on leaving college or died before leaving, and those who left the district. The increase of approximately 15 per cent is due to two factors:

an increase in the severity of handicaps of those entering the Unit resulting in an 8 per cent increase in the unemployable;

lack of jobs accounting for 7 per cent of unemployment amongst leavers.

References

1. Clegg, N.C. (1979) 'Further Education and Training of Handicapped Students – An Integrated Approach at College Level' in K. Dixon and D. Hutchinson (eds) *Further Education for Handicapped Students* (Bolton: Bolton College of Education (Technical))
2. Department of Education and Science (1978) *Special Educational Needs. Report of the Committee of Enquiry into the Education of Handicapped Children and Young People* (The Warnock Report), Cmnd 7212, p. 191 (London: HMSO)
3. Rodger, A. (1951) *The Seven-Point Plan*, Paper No. 1 (London: National Institute of Industrial Psychology)
4. Neale, M.D. (1966) *The Neale Analysis of Reading Ability* (2nd edition) (London: Macmillan)
5. Vernon, P.E. and Miller, K.M. (1976) *Graded Arithmetic-Mathematics Test* (Metric edition) (London: Hodder & Stoughton)
6. Raven, J.C. (1977 edition) *Standard Progressive Matrices* (London: H.K. Lewis)
7. Bennett, G.K., Seashore, H.G. and Wesman, A.G. (1966) *Differential Aptitudes Test* (4th edition) (New York: The Psychological Corporation)
8. Short Clerical Test – Form C (Anglicised edition) (Hawthorn, Victoria: Australian Council for Educational Research)*
9. Clerical Speed and Accuracy Test — Form A (Hawthorn, Victoria: Australian Council for Educational Research)*
10. Mechanical Reasoning Test (1977 edition) (Hawthorn, Victoria: Australian Council for Educational Research)*
11. Bennett, G.K. (1965) *Hand-tool Dexterity Test* (New York: The Psychological Corporation)
12. Crawford, J.E. and Crawford, D.M. (1956) *Small Parts Dexterity Test* (New York: The Psychological Corporation)
13. Tiffin, J. (1948) *Purdue Pegboard* (Chicago: Science Research Associates)
14. Crowley, A.D. (1976) *Occupational Interests Blank* (2nd edition) (Cambridge: CRAC)
15. Hutchinson, D. (1977) *Personal-Occupational Satisfactions Guide* (Worksop: North Nottinghamshire College of Further Education)

16. Daws, P. (1965) 'The Occupational Satisfactions Sought by Fifth Form Pupils', unpublished paper, Vocational Guidance Research Unit, University of Leeds

* Normative data on these tests is available in:
(for 8 and 9) Pintilie, D. and Nyfield, G. (1979) *British Supplement of Norms for Tests used in Clerical Selection* (Windsor: NFER)
(for 10) Nyfield, G. (1979) *British Supplement of Norms for Tests used in Apprentice Selection* (Windsor: NFER)

CHAPTER 4

Conclusion: A Measure of Support

If handicapped young people are to make the best use of the facilities available to them for work preparation, then they will need support from a number of sources. This support will be required not only during the time a student is at college and within that context, he will also need support in the wider community of which he is a part, and continue to do so for the rest of his life.

The aim of support services should be to assist the handicapped person to have as normal a life as possible and to reduce the difference existing between the handicapped and the able-bodied, which is the main source of stigma and often leads to their segregation within the community. The provision of work preparation courses in 'normal' establishments of further education, with adequate support, goes some way towards the objective of the World Health Organisation: 'to create a climate of public opinion which will regard the use of public resources in providing services for the handicapped as a well-justified social investment'.[1] We have already recognised that going to work and earning a living is a societal norm, as relevant to the handicappped as to the able-bodied. But these objectives can only be achieved with a measure of positive support in favour of the handicapped. This is true in times of normal employment prospects, but even more so in the period of economic recession and unemployment we are facing in the 1980s.

The specific areas of support required vary considerably according to the needs of the individual handicapped young person; however, they can be grouped into areas of general relevance.

Information and Advice

For an able-bodied young person the time of leaving school is associated with a vast array of information and, potentially at least, a wide range of job choices. It must be a confusing experience; but more especially for the young person whose problems are compounded with the difficulties of a handicap.

Since many handicaps are relatively low in incidence there is a need to make information available on a national scale. In 1975 the National Bureau for Handicapped Students was formed, partly because there was little organised information as to what was available for handicapped students. In five years the

Bureau has already established itself as a source of information on facilities for handicapped students, including admissions procedures, examination arrangements, specialist curricula, adaptations to buildings, support staff requirements, specialist teaching aids, grants and other financial provision, specialist colleges, accommodation needs, guidance of staff, helpful voluntary agencies, placement, vocational opportunities and statutory agencies, especially relating to careers and employment. In collating and disseminating information, amongst its numerous activities, the Bureau is serving an important function at national (and lately regional) level, and it is regrettable that its source of income from public funds has been extremely limited.

An example of what can be done on a regional basis is provided by the working party on handicapped students, set up by the Regional Advisory Council for the Organisation of Further Education in the East Midlands. A survey of further and higher education in each of the five counties covered by the Regional Advisory Council (Derbyshire, Lincolnshire, Leicestershire, Northamptonshire and Nottinghamshire) was made and published for the information of prospective students and their families.[2] Unfortunately, further plans for the future work of this group have had to be curtailed as a result of the financial cut-backs. For most students, however, information and advice will come from agencies within their own local area. Again, a good working example is provided by the *Handbook on Young People with Special Needs*, published by the Sheffield Area Health Authority (Teaching), which provides information on a wide variety of subjects for handicapped young people.[3]

The important principle lying behind all types and sources of information and advice is that it should be readily available to the consumer, and that maximum publicity should be given as to where help can be obtained.

Careers Advice

The majority of handicapped young people will receive their careers advice from a specialist careers officer for the handicapped, employed by a Local Education Authority; a small minority will be dealt with by careers officers from voluntary organisations, and some young people, perhaps at a later stage, will receive help from a Disablement Resettlement Officer. Whilst the main role of the careers officer is to give advice on employment and training for employment, and assistance in finding a job, it is inevitable that he is called upon to perform duties outside of the normal course of his professional remit. It is not difficult to appreciate why this is so. At school-age the young person and his family will naturally turn, perhaps, to the headteacher or the specialist doctor to provide information or to counsel them in times of difficulty. However, on leaving school, many facets of the care given to a young person change: the familiar headteacher may be replaced by an unknown quantity in the form of a college tutor, and even the familiar paediatrician may be replaced by a different range of adult specialists. The only constant, in most cases, in this transitory phase from school to adult life is the specialist careers officer who has known the young person at school and continues to be responsible for him while he is preparing for work. In suggesting that he should be the 'named person', or single point of contact, for these young people with special needs during this difficult, and sometimes traumatic, period of their life, the Warnock Report recognised the difficulties facing young people with handicaps and the special competence of the Careers Service.[4]

In helping young people prepare for work, particularly in a college situation, the careers adviser is a vital member of the team. The formal role of careers guidance and placement is well defined, but the informal one of counsellor and confidant is not. Yet it is this role which is likely to occupy much of a career officer's time. Our own practices in the Work Orientation Unit recognise this fact and, in addition to being invited to case conferences and reviews, careers officers are encouraged to visit as often as possible to maintain contact with the young people they have referred to us. This process of informal contact is of benefit both ways, for not only is the careers officer able to maintain contact, but also to be of practical assistance to the College by helping in work experience arrangements, or obtaining financial help for the young person from the Department of Health and Social Security, and so on. However, if this important role is to continue, let alone develop, it is essential that the extra load on an already overstretched service is allowed for by those responsible for the Careers Service. As more and more handicapped young people are placed in an increasing variety of training situations, the need for the careers officer to monitor these placements must be recognised in terms of manpower required. Far too often, shortage of time can mean a placement in training is just one less job to do rather than an excellent opportunity to follow up a case over a longer period, noting the changes and developments taking place.

At the same time as careers advice and help is given to young people, this will be rendered less than effective if opportunities for placement are not available. Schemes of public education, such as the Manpower Services Commission's 'Fit to Work' scheme, already referred to, are to be welcomed, as are the efforts of the voluntary organisations in this area of support for handicapped young people. For example, the National Bureau for Handicapped Students has been active in preparing an employment policy statement to complement the earlier one on education. This statement is based upon evidence collected by the Bureau and upon discussion with handicapped people, with industry, commerce and the trade unions, together with central and local government agencies. But if these single efforts are to be of any use they need to be combined so that constant pressure is maintained to educate the public as to the positive benefits of employing handicapped people.

Personal Counselling

'There is a surprising failure to recognise the acute problems of isolation from their peers that confront many of the more seriously handicapped adolescents, who face, often without the chance to satisfy them, the normal urges of young people for companionship, relations with the opposite sex, sport, enjoyment of leisure pursuits, travel, spending money, achievement, and the prospect of their own home and family.'[5]

Warnock, too, says that handicapped young people 'may require advice on a range of personal matters including health, and personal and sexual relationships. Counselling on these subjects needs to be readily available and it should be a function of the "named person" to make the necessary arrangements for a young person with special needs to receive appropriate counselling where this is required.'[6]

It may seem out of place in a text on work preparation for the handicapped to discuss personal counselling and, in particular, sexual relationships. But those with experience of the needs of handicapped young people find this an important area of difficulty, to the extent that attempts to train and educate can be thwarted by the sense of isolation and frustration felt by some adolescents coming to terms with the physical and emotional problems of puberty, compounded by the problem of coming to terms with a handicap. Too often, society, in general, and the professions working with the handicapped, in particular, have not only paid too little attention to the sexual needs of handicapped people but have deliberately ignored the problem. The justification for this has typically been either that the problem does not exist or that nothing can be done about it. The denial of the sexuality of the handicapped means that many of them present as sexual neuters: their handicap has assumed so important a place in their lives that they have little awareness of their male and female roles. Sexuality is so important to personality development that handicapped young people need a full appreciation of themselves as men and women in the society of which they are a part, in so far as their disabilities will allow. Sex education for the handicapped is usually neglected or badly handled, although the subject and its wider aspect of social responsibility warrants more rather than less emphasis in the special school. Handicapped young people have less opportunity for acquiring sexual knowledge experimentally, through self-initiated or peer-initiated activities, due to the limitations of their lives imposed by their own restricted mobility and, therefore, diminished social outlets. Parents also contribute to the problem by frequently overlooking the sexual nature of their handicapped off-spring, or by denying appropriate opportunities for social contact with peers, because they are fearful of the consequences.

Clearly, the young person who is at risk because of lack of sexual knowledge, or who displays unacceptable sexual behaviour, is at a disadvantage in obtaining or retaining employment, even though vocational skills might be at a high level. Handicapped people, like anyone else, are sexual beings; parents and professionals alike have no recourse but to accept this. But, having done so, there is then the obligation to help the young person to develop an appropriate sexual identity, educate him to understand his own sexuality and social responsibility, and help (but allow) him to make his own decisions. Within the Work Orientation Unit we have found that a carefully structured programme of health education, related to personal development and work, has provided the forum in which to discuss not only sexual relationships but also such problems as drug abuse, alcohol and smoking. It has also acted as a catalyst to bring individual personal problems to the forefront, where they can be picked up by the trained counsellor available in the college. The knowledge that this is being done has encouraged parents to come along and discuss their views and difficulties in dealing with their adolescent son or daughter.

It is impossible to draw firm conclusions regarding personal counselling for the handicapped young person because of the variety of needs and characteristics. However, success in this important area depends as much upon positive attitudes as upon the practical details of the services available.

Aids and Financial Assistance

The increase in the number of handicapped young people in training for employment, particularly in further education colleges, has brought with it two other problems in the area of support. First, modern technology has provided a wide range of aids and equipment which can be of use in education and training situations, but as Warnock observes,[7] the dissemination of information on these aids is limited, though the report itself does help by listing the main aids centres known to the Department of Health and Social Security and the Scottish Home and Health Department. Nevertheless, if these developments are to be regarded as part of the wider concept of special educational needs referred to in the Government White Paper *Special Needs in Education*,[8] then a pool of specialist resources should be made available to provide handicapped young people with the aids they need to undertake education and training. In this context, it is also important that training in the use of such aids is given prior to the commencement of a course. Again, aids for handicapped people are a highly individualised matter covering such areas as tools, adaptations to machines and furniture, as well as aids for reading and writing, communication and mobility. A particular problem may require many different solutions and the best people to tackle the problem may be those in the college or training establishment itself. However, when a student leaves college, these services must also follow on into employment, and the facility provided currently by the Employment Service

Agency in supplying aids to individual handicapped people and to employers needs to be more widely publicised and expanded. The organisation of the supply of aids is far from satisfactory and, according to the case, the same type of aid can be provided by the Local Education Authority, by the Social Services Department or by the Health Authority. This is a waste of scarce resources at a time when they are needed to expand the service and can result in aids not being provided because a particular agency is not satisfied that a need really exists within their terms of reference. Similarly, co-operation and co-ordination between agencies is required, not just at the level of provision of individual aids, but also in the general provision of access to buildings, adequacy of parking places, and so on.

The area of financial support for handicapped young people undertaking work preparation courses is both disparate and confused. Those whose work is at a residential training college funded by the Training Services Division, or who are supported by the Youth Opportunities Programme, are considerably better provided for than those whose course is at a local FE college. These students, at best, may receive non-contributory invalidity benefit or supplementary benefit from the Department of Health and Social Security or, at worst, have to rely on an educational maintenance grant. Warnock[9] recommended that local authorities should help handicapped students by making use of their discretionary powers in awarding grants but, in the two years since the report was published, there has been little evidence of this taking place. It has also become more difficult to obtain financial benefits from the DHSS because of the often rigid application of eligibility criteria in respect of certain handicapped groups. In reviewing the legal framework governing further education, which currently does not make specific reference to the needs of handicapped students,[10] it is to be hoped that the existing disparity between education and vocational training in financial terms is removed.

It is perhaps the attitude towards financial support for the handicapped, whether in training or not, that encapsulates public attitudes towards the handicapped in general. One criterion for judging a society is the way in which it looks after its less fortunate members. The level of financial support to handicapped students preparing for work in the United Kingdom suggests that the attitude of our society leaves much to be desired. Reference has already been made to the philosophy of the World Health Organisation, which talks of 'justifiable social investment'. At a more pragmatic level, Cooke (1979) talks of a 'pay now, save later' theme in giving the kind of help required to assist handicapped young people 'to achieve the maximum degree of personal development, self-fulfilment, social responsibility and independence'.[11] Whichever standpoint is preferred, the end product is likely to be the same, and the change of attitude required to bring it about just as great.

References

1. World Health Organisation (1967) *Report of a Working Group on the Early Detection and Treatment of Handicapping Defects in Young Children* (Copenhagen: Regional Office for Europe, WHO)
2. Regional Advisory Council for the Organisation of Further Education in the East Midlands (1980-81) *Further Education for Handicapped People* (2nd edition) (Nottingham: Regional Advisory Council for the Organisation of Further Education in the East Midlands)
3. Sheffield Area Health Authority (Teaching) (1978) *Young People with Special Needs*, The Sheffield Handbook (Sheffield Area Health Authority (Teaching))
4. Department of Education and Science (1978) *Special Educational Needs. Report of the Committee of Enquiry into the Education of Handicapped Children and Young People* (The Warnock Report), Cmnd 7212, p. 191 (London: HSMO)
5. Younghusband, E., Burchall, D., Davie, R. and Pringle, M.L.K. (eds) (1970) *Living with Handicap* (London: National Bureau for Co-operation in Child Care)
6. The Warnock Report (1978) pp. 191-2
7. The Warnock Report (1978) pp. 198-9
8. Department of Education and Science (1980) *Special Needs in Education*, Government White Paper, Cmnd 7996, para. 52 (London: HMSO)
9. The Warnock Report (1978) pp. 194-6
10. Department of Education and Science (1980) *Special Needs in Education*, Cmnd 7996, para. 52
11. Cooke, G.V. (1979) 'The Implications of Warnock for Further Education' in K. Dixon and D. Hutchinson (eds) *Further Education for Handicapped Students* (Bolton: Bolton College of Education (Technical))

APPENDIX ONE

THE RANGE OF VOCATIONAL TRAINING COURSES AVAILABLE AT THE FOUR RESIDENTIAL TRAINING COLLEGES

College	Course	Duration
1. Portland Training College, Mansfield	Elementary Business Studies	20 weeks
	Intermediate Business Studies	20 weeks
	Electronic Wiring and Assembly	13 weeks
	Industrial Electronics	26 weeks
	Radio, Television and Electronics Servicing	52 weeks
	Electro/Mechanical Craft	39 weeks
	Horology	52 weeks
	Horticulture	52 weeks
2. Finchale Training College, Durham	Horticulture	52 weeks
	Typewriter Mechanics	52 weeks
	Watch and Clock Repairs	52 weeks
	Bench Joinery	26 weeks
	Domestic Service Engineers	26 weeks
	Business Studies	26 weeks
	Machine Operating	15 weeks
	Assistant Quantity Surveyors	39 weeks
3. Queen Elizabeth's Training College, Leatherhead	Bench Joinery	26 weeks
	Builders Quantities	39 weeks
	Business Studies — Standard Course	30 weeks
	Advanced Course (additional)	12 weeks
	Computer Programming	12 weeks
	Electric Arc Welding	30 weeks
	Engineering Draughtsmanship	39 weeks
	Gardening	52 weeks
	Light Electrical Servicing	26 weeks
	Reception	26 weeks
	Spray Painting	26 weeks
	Telephone Switchboard Operating	13 weeks
	Typing — Shorthand/Typing	39 weeks
	Speedwriting/Typing	26 weeks
	Audio Typing	26 weeks

	Copy Typing	16 weeks
4. St Loye's Training College, Exeter	Book-keeping and Accounts	32 weeks
	Industrial Cookery	26 weeks
	Data Preparation	26 weeks
	Electronics Servicing	52 weeks
	Electronic Wiring	20 weeks
	Engineering Inspection	20 weeks
	Horticulture	52 weeks
	Hotel Reception	32 weeks
	Joinery	26 weeks
	Light Electro-mechanical Fitting	36 weeks
	Light Precision Engineering	36 weeks
	Radio and Television Servicing	52 weeks
	Copy/Audio/Shorthand Typing	22, 26, 45 weeks
	Storekeeping	14 weeks
	Telephony/Reception/Typing	18 weeks
	Watch and Clock Repair	52 weeks

SIGNIFICANT LIVING WITHOUT WORK: A COURSE FOR THE SEVERELY HANDICAPPED

1. Course Aims

To prepare those students for whom employment in either open or sheltered terms will be an unlikely prospect, to approach the future in a purposeful and creative manner so that their lives have significance and personal satisfaction.

2. Objectives

(1) To develop the student's potential for independence in the activities of daily living.
(2) To develop the student's potential for independent mobility.
(3) To develop the student's enthusiasm and responsibility for learning as far as his/her interests dictate and understanding warrants, emphasis being placed on utilitarian knowledge and learning with a social base.
(4) To improve the student's communication skills.
(5) To provide counselling, on a one-to-one basis where necessary, and group discussion where appropriate, of matters related to disability and to personal relationships and emotional development.
(6) To provide group discussion of current affairs and stimulate interest in national and world affairs.
(7) To determine and develop the student's recreational interests and creative skills to the point where they can be pursued out of college.
(8) To make the student fully aware of the services for handicapped people which his/her local community offers and to foster integration into those which are acceptable and beneficial to him/her.

3. Selection of Students

Initial assessment will consist of obtaining information in the following areas:

Physical fitness
Mobility
Manual dexterity
Educational attainment

Academic potential
Recreational interests and skills
Future plans

The first month of the course should be regarded as probationary so that a final assessment of the suitability of the course for each student can be made.

4. *Number of Students*

A maximum of 10 students per year of course.

5. *Timetable*

36 weeks per year of course.
30 hours per week, but may vary to suit individual student needs.

6. *Areas of Education*

The 30 hours per week will be split as follows:

(a) Social education/community activities/mobility exercises/personal care/counselling	8 hours
(b) General education	6 hours
(c) Recreational activities	4 hours
(d) Domestic cookery	3 hours
(e) PE/wheelchair sports	3 hours
(f) Placement, e.g. Social Services Day Centre	6 hours

7. *Course Content*

(Modified according to student's needs and potential after assessment.)

A. *Social Education/Community Activities/Mobility Exercises/Personal Care/ Counselling.* Many of these skills should be practised in the student's home locality with the involvement of the student's tutor wherever necessary. Among the topics which could be listed, the following could be considered paramount.

Social education
Establish and maintain relationships.
Give and get satisfaction from relationships.
Tolerate rebukes and opposition.
Show normal responses to kindness and affection.

Possess basic communication skills.

Social graces — please and thank you, etc.

Initiate a conversation. Make introductions.

Awareness of 'moves' relating to sexual behaviour.

Use telephone. Telephone directory. Directory enquiries. Emergency calls.

Seek advice.

Handle money.

Use cafes, restaurants, etc.

Make and keep appointments. Letter writing. Form filling.

Punctuality. Tell the time.

Awareness of functions of aspects of Public Services — Police, Hospitals, Health Centres, Social Services.

Awareness of dangers in excessive smoking/drinking/drugs.

Community activities

Join clubs and societies open to the general public.

Use cinemas, theatres, pubs and other places of entertainment.

Ability to dance?

Use of day centres and PHAB club facilities and activities.

Use libraries and museums.

Mobility exercises

Use of public transport, both local and further afield. Handle fares and timetables.

Wheelchair activites:

> propel forward
> turn
> use brakes
> propel on uneven ground
> mount kerb
> descend kerb
> propel up slope
> propel down slope
> cross street at traffic lights
> wheelchair to toilet
> toilet to wheelchair
> open and close doors
> reach floor
> wheelchair to car
> car to wheelchair

Use of invacar. Driving and general management.

Use of sticks, crutches, aids:

> walking on even ground

> walking on uneven ground
> walking up slope
> walking down slope
> mounting kerbs/stairs
> descending kerbs/stairs

Personal care

Bath, wash, shave.

Care of hair, teeth, nails.

Change and disposal of sanitary towels.

Use public toilets.

Dress, choose and maintain clothes — suitability of dress for different occasions. Recognise colours.

Pack a suitcase, estimating needs.

Undertake basic domestic tasks. House cleaning:

> sweep floor
> vacuum clean
> polish, dust
> clean sink, bath, toilet
> make bed

Simple washing/ironing/mending. Use of washing machine/spin drier.

How to ask for, follow and give simple directions.

Save money, e.g. Post Office Book, Savings Stamps, Bank.

Use of stamps. Post Office.

Take precautions against fire hazards. Safety notices.

Simple first aid. Take medicine under direction.

Set an alarm clock.

Counselling

Areas to be covered would include:

Problems of developing a handicapped identity.

Growing up with a disability.

Social integration.

Personal relationships/emotional development.

Community attitudes.

Disability and assisted independence.

Current affairs — local, national, world.

Topics chosen by group's members.

B. *General Education.* Individually prepared programmes will be designed for each student.

Literacy

The aim will be to extend the student's sight, spoken and written vocabularies, applied to:

(1) Furtherance of social development: letter writing, telegrams, telephones, directions, newspapers, magazines, clubs and societies, current affairs, use of library and civic information services.
(2) Management of everyday activities: travel, timetables, maps, holiday arrangements, paying bills, application forms, writing name and address, sight reading of socially valuable words, seeking assistance, etc.
(3) Development of personal interests: hobbies, academic interests, literature and 'knowledge for its own sake', stimulating and satisfying intellectual curiosity via the expressive arts, sciences and humanities.

Numeracy
The aim will be to develop the student's knowledge and appreciation of the four rules of number, simple measurement, decimalisation and metrication, applied to:

(1) Furtherance of social development: costs of entertainment and leisure activities.
(2) Management of everyday activities: cost of food, travel, savings, interest, hire purchase, insurance bills, cost of private transport, etc.
(3) Development of personal interests: costs of hobbies, recreational activities, academic interests, etc.
C. *Recreational Activities:* A wide range of activities will be available including art, handicrafts such as embroidery, sewing, collage, model-making, drawing, pottery, photography, film-making, musical appreciation, drama — involving listening/watching using radio/film/television and active participation to whatever degree the disability allows.
D. *Domestic Cookery.* Areas to be covered will include:

Use of gas and electric cookers and meter.
Open cooker doors and move shelves.
Lift dishes in and out of oven.
Use basic cooking utensils. Lifting and filling kettle and saucepans at tap.
Opening tins.
Preparing and cooking simple meals. Following a recipe.
Cutting bread/spreading butter, etc.
Peeling vegetables.
Washing up/wiping up.
E. *Physical Education/Wheelchair Sports.* Physical exercises to whatever degree the disability allows. Swimming. Use of trampoline. Wheelchair races. Table-tennis, ball games, archery, fencing, etc.
F. *Placement.* It is recognised that a full-time placement in the college can only last for a limited period, after which a placement in a Social Services establishment will be required. However, very few young people recognise this type of placement as an acceptable step upon leaving school. The

purpose, therefore, of the placement scheme is to introduce the students to those agencies who will be responsible for their care in the long term.

Initially, a placement will be for one day per week, either in the first or the second year of the course, depending on the student's needs. This will be extended as time progresses to the point where the young person is placed in another establishment and attends college on a limited basis, for example on day release or to attend part-time courses of, say, adult education.

Close co-operation in the organisation of this scheme is maintained with the Social Services Department and other agencies.

APPENDIX THREE

SPECIMEN PAGES FROM THE APPLICATION FORM

Section A: General Information

Section D: Medical Information
D1 Physically Handicapped
D2 Visually Handicapped
D4 Epilepsy

Section E: Vocational Information

SECTION A (to be completed by the last school attended) <u>GENERAL INFORMATION</u>

SURNAME_____CHRISTIAN NAME/S_____

ADDRESS _____

_____ Tel. No. _____

DATE OF BIRTH _____

SCHOOLS ATTENDED _____
(Past 5 years)
_____

_____

NAME OF PARENT/GUARDIAN _____OCCUPATION _____

NATURE OF DISABILITY/HANDICAP OF APPLICANT _____

ANY OTHER DISABILITIES/HANDICAPS _____

(Please complete the appropriate form(s) in Section D for each disability,
however slight it may be).

<u>PHYSICAL DEVELOPMENT</u>

Height : short/medium/tall

Build : slight/medium/well built/overweight

Speech : normal/slight impairment/difficult to understand

<u>SELF CARE</u>
Completely independent/needs some help _____

Indicate degree of help needed _____

<u>ABILITY TO USE PUBLIC TRANSPORT</u>

Independent/accompanied/not at all

Has own transport/uses invalid car

<u>FOR COLLEGE USE ONLY</u>

DATE APPLICATION FORM RECEIVED _____

INTERVIEW DATE _____

PRESENT AT INTERVIEW _____

ACTION/DATE _____

BASIS OF ACCEPTANCE _____

TRIAL PERIOD _____ WEEKS

1 YEAR _____

2 YEARS _____

DATE OF ENTRY TO COLLEGE _____

SECTION D (to be completed by the relevant medical   MEDICAL INFORMATION
            officer or by the school from current records)

D.1.   PHYSICALLY HANDICAPPED

Nature of Handicap

Cause: Congenital/Accident/Other _____

_____

Severity: Slight/Moderate/Very Severe _____

_____

Duration: _____

Mobility   Walks Independently - Normally/Steadily/Unsteadily

           Walks with aid   - Crutches/Calipers/Walking Frame/Other

           Wheelchair   - Independent Indoors & Outdoors/
                                     Short Distance/Indoors Only

Comments _____

_____

_____

Self Care: Dressing - Independent/Needs Help/Totally Dependent

           _____

           Toilet - Independent/Needs Help/Totally Dependent

           _____

Use of Hands: Limited/Normal/Can Use One Hand Only/No Effective Use

           _____

Writing Skills: No Handwriting/Limited Handwriting/Normal Handwriting/
                Manual Typewriting/Electric Typewriting

           _____

Other Relevant Information:

_____

_____

_____

_____

_____

_____

D.2. VISUALLY HANDICAPPED

Nature of Sight Condition: _____

_____

Cause (If Known): _____

Duration: _____

Amount of Sight

(a) Without Glasses : Left Eye _____ Right Eye _____

(b) With Glasses   : Left Eye _____ Right Eye _____

Registered As: Blind Person/Partially Sighted/Neither

_____

Colour Blindness: State Which Colours _____

_____

Night Blindness: Yes/No _____

Degree _____

Visual Aids Used: Reading _____

Writing _____

Knowledge of
Braille   : Reading _____

Writing _____

Knowledge of   : Manual _____
Touch Typing
Electric _____

Mobility :   Completely Independent/Independent In Own Environment/
Independent Indoors Only

_____

Is Condition Likely to: Improve/Remain Stationary/Deteriorate

_____

Other Relevant Information: _____

_____

_____

_____

_____

_____

D.4. <u>EPILEPSY</u>

Degree of Disablement _____

Duration of Disablement _____

Date of first signs _____

Is the Applicant still subject to fits? _____

Is the epilepsy well controlled? _____

_____

Are Drugs Prescribed?   Yes/No

If Yes: Drugs _____ Dosage _____

Do they have any side effects? _____

_____

Frequency of Fits _____

Date of Last Fit _____

Do they occur at regular intervals? _____

Do they occur whilst awake, asleep or both?

_____

Is any factor known to precipitate the fits?   Yes/No

If Yes: What are the warning signs? _____

_____

_____

How long before the fit do they occur? _____

_____

How long do the fits normally last? _____

What form do they take? _____

_____

What is the nature and duration of any after effects? _____

_____

_____

Is there any disturbance of behaviour or any personality problem?

_____

_____

_____

_____

SECTION E (to be completed by the referring   VOCATIONAL INFORMATION
                careers officer)

Previous Employment (If Any) _____

_____

Applicant's Preference for Employment _____

_____

_____

Which of these, if any, are within the Applicant's potential?

(a) As of Now _____

_____

(b) Given Suitable Education/Training _____

_____

Action Recommended to Enable Applicant to Attain Vocational Preferences:

(a) Social/Educational _____

_____

(b) Vocational _____

_____

From Which Occupation Would Applicant be Excluded Because of Disability? :

_____

_____

Type of Occupation Ultimately Envisaged: _____

_____

Interview Notes. Personality, Attitude to Work: _____

_____

_____

_____

Parental Attitude to Employment etc.: _____

_____

_____

Name of Referring Careers Officer: _____

Local Authority _____

Tel. No.: _____

APPENDIX FOUR

PRACTICAL SOCIAL SKILLS CHECK-LIST

NAME .... AGE .... DATE OF BIRTH .... TUTORIAL GROUP ....

Each item is rated on a scale: **5 4 3 2 1**

SELF HELP

Item	5	4	3	2	1
Completes toilet inc. hair, teeth, nails, washing, etc.					
Dresses adequately inc. choice of clothes, according to weather.					
Finds own way. Goes errands.					
Uses Public Transport.					
Can use time-tables, maps, etc.					

COMMUNICATION

Item	5	4	3	2	1
Relates events in an understanding way.					
Remembers and delivers messages.					
Answers telephone sensibly.					
Uses Public telephone.					
Recognises coins and knows values.					
Can receive and translate written instructions.					
Adds simple sums					
Tells time and associates with actions or events					
Understands time intervals. Knows 24 hr clock.					
Able to use ruler or measuring table.					
Recognises social sight vocabulary & understands.					
Can write formal and informal letters.					
Able to read simple printed matter.					
Can repeat, recognise and write name and address.					
Addresses envelope - write simple letter.					
Fill in main items on application form.					
Manners and co-operation with others.					

Social Integration Competence — Social attitudes and abilities

Item	5	4	3	2	1
Makes purchases in supermarkets. Buys from shops.					
Buys own clothes and knows sizes. Does minor repairs.					
Helps in the home - cleaning, dish-washing.					
Able to prepare snack meals.					
Able to cook a meal using tins and frozen foods.					
Basic understanding of the law. Legal rights. Hire Purchase, etc.					

Finance and Initiative

Item	5	4	3	2	1
Knows postage rates for letters and where to obtain licenses, etc.					
Saves money to some purpose by Post Office/ other bank.					
Understands and uses simple budget.					
Understands wage deductions.					
Makes and keeps appointments with doctor, dentist, hospital, etc.					

WORK PERFORMANCE

Item	5	4	3	2	1
Application to work - regarding supervision.					
Quantity and accuracy of work.					
Speed and output.					
Time-keeping					
Care of tools and materials.					

Progressive Scale of Assessment
Grade should be shaded in RED

5 = Bottom of scale of achievement
1 = Top of scale of achievement

JOB CARD AND FOLLOW-UP TASKS

Figure A.1: Easy-joints Job Card

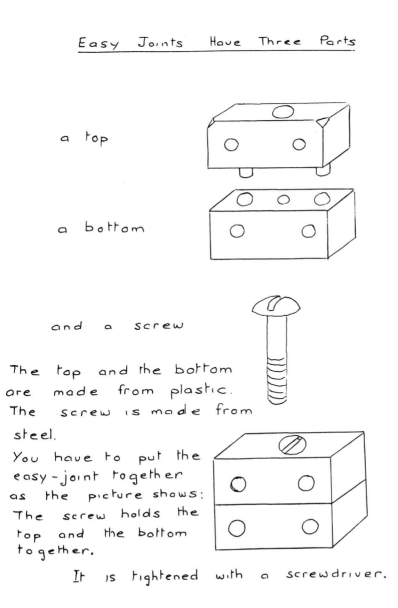

Easy Joints Have Three Parts

a top

a bottom

and a screw

The top and the bottom
are made from plastic.
The screw is made from
steel.
You have to put the
easy-joint together
as the picture shows:
The screw holds the
top and the bottom
together.

It is tightened with a screwdriver.

NAME   GROUP

DAY   DATE   MONTH

THE DAY'S WORK

(1)   Write in the space provided the number of hours work that you did:

      between starting work
      and the morning break   _____

      between the morning break
      and lunch time   _____

      between lunch time
      and the afternoon break   _____

      between the afternoon break
      and finishing work   _____

    The total amount of work =   _____

    The number of credits earned =   _____

(2)   Copy in here the times from
     your clock card:

IN	OUT	IN	OUT

(3)   How many parts does an easy-joint have?

_____

(4) What are the parts made from?

_____

_____

(5) What colour are the parts?

_____

_____

(6) How many easy-joints did you make in :

    (a) One day? _____

    (b) Per hour? _____

(7) What did you exchange your credits for?

_____

_____

(8) Who did you work with?

_____

_____

APPENDIX SIX

GENERAL OPERATIVES BUILDING TRADES COURSE

Duration

Four days per week (24 hrs) over 36 weeks.

Aims of Course

To promote interest in general building work.
To create team spirit within the group.
To encourage a sense of responsibility within the group.
To develop any special aptitudes recognised.

Course Structure

Emphasis on practical project work and site assimilation with related knowledge applicable to and as an extension of the project. Calculations and theory adjusted to suit the ability of the students. Safety and cleanliness stressed at all stages during the course. Classwork lessons to be structured so as to encourage student participation and discussion. Every effort made to encourage participation by all individual students.

Syllabus

Preliminary Operations

Demolition, site clearance. Temporary roads. Temporary services, water, electricity to site. Site buildings. WC and welfare buildings, offices and storage sheds and erection of same. Temporary fences, hoardings, notice boards and signs. Formation of entrance to site and provision of temporary roads. Form storage areas in preparation for materials deliveries.

Safety

Personal safety, including use of protective clothing. Safety in the use of hand tools and powered tools. General site safety, regard for others; importance of site tidiness. Machinery, moving parts, loose clothing and the danger thereof. Particular regard to safety in excavation, demolition and scaffolding.

Excavation

Hand and mechanical methods. Tools used in excavation. Safety hazards in deep excavation, simple planking and strutting. Return fill and ram by hand and by mechanical means. Control of ground water during excavation. Relate this topic to 'safety' above.

Measurement, Setting Out, Reading Drawings

Types of measuring equipment available. Use of metric units. Use of pegs, lines, profile boards, range rods and boning rods. Setting out right angle by using 3-4-5 method and by using builders square. Measurement of diagonals as check for square in a rectangle. Introduction to simple levelling techniques using level and straight edge. Simple levelling with Cowley level. Reading simple drawings.

Site Discipline

Site supervision staff structure — General Foreman, Foreman, Tradesmen, Labourers, Professional and Inspection Staff, Clerk of Works, Building Inspector. The building regulations. Safety Inspector, the safety regulations. Recording of accidents. Timekeeping, swearing, smoking, insubordination. Working hours. Care of employer's materials, plant, equipment and property.

Calculations

Addition, subtraction, multiplication of decimals with emphasis on application to building. Calculation of total running lengths. Calculation of simple rectangular shaped areas and volumes in mm^2, mm^3, m^2 and m^3. All calculations to be related to simple building plan and section.

Concrete Practice

Materials used, coarse aggregate, fine aggregate and cement. Silt test. Cleanliness of water used. Mixing concrete by hand and by machine. Consistency, workability and strength of concrete. Making and testing standard cubes. Water cement ratio and its effect on strength. Simple moulds and formwork. Transporting and placing concrete on site. Protection in wet weather. Curing in dry weather. Effect of frost. Surface finishes.

Drainage

Regulations affecting the construction of domestic drains. Testing drains. Identification of various salt glazed pipes and fittings. Manhole construction, channel, pipe jointing, laying, levelling. Cutting pipes of various types. Flexible drainware joints. Pitch fibre pipes, plastic drains. Stacking and storage of drainware.

Brickwork

Mortars, gauging, mixing, transporting of various types, use of hods, barrows, etc. Sands of various types and their uses, plasticisers, lime mortars. Use of trowel, spreading of mortar. Mortar spots. Setting out for bricklayer. Bonding brickwork, footings, setting out, DPCs, levels, gauge or storey rods. Loading, unloading and stacking of bricks. Jointing and finishes.

Scaffolding

Erection and preparation of working platforms. Simple tubular scaffolds complete with toeboards and guard rails. Identification and maintenance of scaffold fittings. Mobile scaffold tower. Use and care of trestles and planks. Ladders — use and maintenance. Safety requirement applicable to scaffolding, hoists, trestles, ladders, etc.

Plumbing

Tools explained and methods of assisting plumbers in fitting copper pipes, bending and cutting steel tubes, threading, etc. Holes cut for pipes in walls, etc. Unloading and stacking or storage of sanitary ware and glass.

Plastering

Tools and equipment, care of, etc. Mixing of various mortars, gauging and mixing of various plasters. Handling plasterboards, cutting and fixing methods. Expanded metal angle beads, use and fixing. Safe storage of plastering materials.

Carpentry and Joinery

Definition of trade and description of work covered by the trade. Typical sizes of, method of support and handling of floor joists. Types of and fixing of floor boarding. Unloading, stacking and protection of carpentry and joinery materials. Effects of moisture, and of incorrect stacking on timber and joinery. Care of carpenters' and joiners' tools.

Painting

Reasons: protection, appearance, advertisement. Knotting and priming to joinery, types of primers and their uses. Importance of moisture content when painting timber. Care of kettles, brushes and other materials. Cleaning and painting site equipment and temporary site buildings.

APPENDIX SEVEN

ENGINEERING LIMITED SKILLS COURSE LOG-BOOK

TRAINING LOG BOOK

FOR

BASIC ENGINEERING SKILLS

NAME -

TUTOR GROUP -

W.O.U.

N.N.C.F.E.

PURPOSE OF LOG BOOK

(1) To provide a record of training and performance.

   This record will be assessed towards a successful conclusion
   of the course.

(2) To record the details of the tasks - work pieces performed,
   in the form of notes and sketches.

(3) Log book to be kept up to date by the student.

FORM OF TRAINING	DATE STARTED	DATE COMPLETED	LECTURERS INITIALS
FIRST YEAR			
BASIC SKILLS			
BENCH WORK			
—			
MACHINE WORK			
—			
RELATED STUDIES TECHNICAL DRG.			

NOTTINGHAMSHIRE COUNTY COUNCIL: EDUCATION COMMITTEE
NORTH NOTTINGHAMSHIRE COLLEGE OF FURTHER EDUCATION

SYLLABUS FOR COURSE:

WORK ORIENTATION BASIC ENGINEERING SKILLS

DURATION OF COURSE -

The students to spend approximately 17 hours per week in the engineering
workshops for a period of 28 weeks. If after this period it is felt
that he is benefiting from this course, a further 22 weeks course should
be pursued.

AIMS OF COURSE

(a)   to attempt a diagnosis of the student's
      suitability for employment in an engineering
      environment.

(b)   To motivate and increase the student's
      enthusiasm to succeed.

(c)   To make every endeavour to try and find an
      engineering outlet for the successful
      student(s) of this course.

SUGGESTED WORK PIECES FOR THE WORK ORIENTATION LIMITED SKILLS COURSE

1. Drill gauge - (possible first exercise)

2. Hand vice

3. Cold chisels - large and small size

4. Centre punch and scriber

5. Turning exercise (simple)

6. Screw-driver (medium size 150 mm blade)

7. Tap wrench

8. Junior hacksaw

9. Adjustable spanner

10. Plumb bob

11. Tool box No. 1 (basic)

12. Trammels

13. Screw-driver (heavy duty)*

14. Hand vice - with handle *

15. Tool box No. 2 (advanced)*

16. Scribing block (round base)*

17. Hammer*

18. Try square*

19. Pipe wrench*

20. Ratchet spanner*

* suggested second level work

The following is intended as an outline of a Syllabus for Work Orientation Students who are considered suitable and who wish to be taught Basic Engineering Skills.

DEMONSTRATION FOLLOWED BY CLOSELY SUPERVISED PRACTICE	RELATED KNOWLEDGE
1. GENERAL FITTING AND BENCH DRILLING Use of rule, dividers, calipers, scribers, surface gauge, punches, hammer, hacksaw, square and file. Marking off and filing to wide limits. Introduction to the drilling machine and chucks. Drilling practice; through holes in mild steel, etc.	Safety precautions as applied to fitting. Explanation of hand tools and care in using them. Classification of files, drills, chisels. Safety in the use of drilling machines. Lubrication and cutting oil.
2. GENERAL FITTING AND BENCH DRILLING Further drilling practice; through and blind holes in sheet and plate, etc; simple template marking, part mating and hole spacing. Filing flat and square. Practice in use of micrometer. Filing, marking-out and drilling to closer limits.	Care and safety in using off-hand grinders. Types of drilling machines and uses; types and range of twist drills and uses; drilling feeds and speeds. Centring, starting and correcting inaccurate starts. Correct holding, clamping and locating. Use of micrometer.
3. GENERAL FITTING AND DRILLING Drilling and tapping; hand taps. Counter-sinking and counter boring. Stud and pin fitting; hand and machine reamers. Plug gauges. Filing, chipping, marking-out, sawing, etc.	Screw threads, tapping drills and tapping. Screws and their uses. Other fastening and locking devices. Limit systems and gauges. Common metals; their properties and uses.
4. GENERAL FITTING Hand scraping of flat surfaces. Marking out and drilling of holes on pitch circle diameter. Detail fitting and assembly exercise entailing use of all practices to date.	Metric system of measurement. Imperial system of measurement.
5. SHAPING Demonstration of the operation of the shaping machine. Practice in work-holding methods. Shaping sides of matching plates. Shaping plates to size and thickness. Shaping squares and cubes.	Safety precautions as applied to the shaping machine. Lubrication. The quick-return movement. Cutting tools used for shaping.

-2-

DEMONSTRATION FOLLOWED BY CLOSELY SUPERVISED PRACTICE	RELATED KNOWLEDGE
6. CENTRE LATHE TURNING Introduction to centre lathe. Practice in the use of lathe controls. Introduction to plain turning – rough cuts only. Plain facing in steps and varying depths of cuts. Turning and facing stepped diameters in three-jaw chuck to open limits, using rule and firm joint calipers for checking.	Safety precautions as applied to centre lathe turning. The Centre Lathe, description, essential features and uses. Work-holding and centring. Tool-holding and centring.
7. CENTRE LATHE TURNING Turning, chamfering, and under-cutting to rule and calipers. Turning stepped diameters to open limits using rule and calipers for checking. Plain turning between centres to open limits. Use of micrometer for checking. Stepped turning and under-cutting to close limits. Finish turning stepped shaft between centres to close limits. Tapping and dieing.	Cutting angles and rakes. Surface and texture. The micrometer and the measuring of turned parts. Centring workpieces. Machine and hand reamers.
8. HEAT TREATMENT Hardening carbon steel, case hardening mild steel, annealing and normalising.	Safety when dealing with hot metals. Types of carbon steel.
9. MILLING MACHINES Only at the discretion of the lecturer concerned - re: ability of the student.	

WORK EXPERIENCE SCHEME

General Aim

To enable students in the Work Orientation Unit, for whom it is considered relevant, to participate in a period of industrial experience as part of their preparation for employment.

Consultation with the Careers Service

(1) The selection of establishments undertaking the employment of students will be made in co-operation with the Careers Officer of the area of placement.
(2) Each firm or establishment used will have been selected with the Careers Officer concerned and the employer made fully aware of the student's background.

Duration

(1) The student will be expected to fulfil the normal requirements of an employee, but consideration will be given to the individual nature of the student's handicap.
(2) It is expected that each student will sample at least two different types of employment while on course in the College.
(3) Those students who will not benefit from a placement outside the College initially, will be given the benefit of undertaking work experience within the College environment as a preliminary to undertaking outside work experience.
(4) The time spent with each employer will depend upon the progress made by the student.

Supervision and Monitoring of Students

(1) Each student will be visited at the place of employment by the member of staff responsible for the placement. The frequency of visits in the initial stages will be fortnightly; as time progresses this will be monthly but could

remain at a more frequent level if the placement requires it.

(2) The views of the employer and the student regarding the placement will be recorded.

Preparation and Follow-up

(1) Employers will be made aware of the philosophy of the scheme and will know the background of the student and the follow-up procedure.

(2) Students will be informed about the place of work, the nature of the work to be undertaken, the hours of work and other requirements of the employer.

(3) Follow-up work experience placements will be undertaken as part of group work in formal work induction classes, but it may also be necessary to undertake individual tutorials with a student regarding various problems.

Selection of Students

(1) The students selected to take part in the Work Experience Scheme will be those who it is considered will benefit from the experience of 'work sampling' in an industrial environment.

(2) In the selection procedure note will be taken of tutor's reports and case conference recommendations. In this process due regard will be paid to the medical problems associated with the individual student handicaps.

Parental Consent

(1) Parents will be made aware of the scheme and its implications.

(2) The written consent of parents will be required on an overall coverage basis before a student takes part in the scheme.

Progress Reports and Discipline

(1) Reports of progress from the person supervising the student within the employment situation will be received, and recommendations made.

(2) Any student found to contravene the employer's or College regulations will be withdrawn from the scheme and may be subject to the College disciplinary process. This particular aspect will apply to any contravention of Health and Safety requirements.

Payment to Students

Students will not receive payment for the work undertaken; they may, however, benefit from any schemes available to normal employees, e.g. free meals.

USEFUL TEXTS FOR SOCIAL AND BASIC EDUCATION PROGRAMMES

Since this whole area is well documented, especially with regard to literacy and numeracy, there is little point in producing long lists here. However, the following texts have been found to be useful in designing programmes for Level Three students.

Blythe, J., Bruce, D. and Henry T. (1978) *Teaching Social and Life Skills* (London: Association for Liberal Education)

Brennan, W.K. and Tansley, A.E. (1976) *School Leaver Series* (Leeds: E.J. Arnold)

Childwall Project (1973) *Design for Living* (Leeds: E.J. Arnold)

Community Services Volunteers (1979) *Life Skills Training Manual* (London: Community Services Volunteers)

Dobinson, H.M. (1979) *Basic Skills You Need* (Sunbury-on-Thames: Nelson)
———— (1979) *Practice in Basic Skills* (Sunbury-on-Thames: Nelson)

Hamblin, D.H. (1977) *The Teacher and Pastoral Care* (Oxford: Basil Blackwell)

Hopson, B. and Scally, M. (1980) *Lifeskills Teaching Programmes*, No. 1 (Leeds: Life Skills Associates)
———— (1981) *Lifeskills Teaching* (Maidenhead: McGraw-Hill)

Howden, R. and Dowson, H. (1979) *The School-leaver's Handbook* (Richmond, Surrey: Careers Consultants)

Lambert, K. (1969) *Life in Our Society*, Books 1-4 (Sunbury-on-Thames: Nelson)

Livock, P. (1982) *Sex Education for the Mentally Handicapped* (London: Croom Helm)

About the Author

David Hutchinson has been Head of the Work Orientation Unit at the North Nottinghamshire College of Further Education since 1970. His pioneering work for handicapped young people has gained him national and international recognition. Co-opted as a member of the Warnock Committee, he is also a member of the Education Commission for Rehabilitation International, as well as a number of other associations at national level. He has travelled extensively to lecture on work preparation and further education for the handicapped in both the UK and abroad.

Index

Leaving school can signal the start of a whole new range of problems for the handicapped. Yet there is a real lack of awareness of the services available to handicapped school leavers, and an inability on the part of educationalists and others to identify the special needs and problems of this group.

This book attempts to remedy this situation, and suggests ways of improving the opportunities of these school leavers. It begins by describing services available, and examines communication between school and post-school levels of provision. It goes on to discuss curriculum development in further education, stressing the need to develop vocational and social skills, and to discriminate between those who will be able to work in the traditional sense and those who cannot hope to do so. Technical aids and teaching/learning resources are then described at length, before the final chapter which briefly assesses the role of support agencies.

David Hutchinson is Head of the Work Orientation Unit at the North Nottinghamshire College of Further Education, Worksop.

CROOM HELM SPECIAL EDUCATION SERIES

Edited by Bill Gillham, Child Development Research Unit, University of Nottingham

CONTENTS

£6.95 net
in UK only

ISBN 0-7099-0283-2